HERMES BOOKS

John Herington, General Editor

VIRGIL

DAVID R. SLAVITT

YALE UNIVERSITY PRESS
NEW HAVEN AND LONDON

Set in Palatino Roman by Brevis Press, Bethany, Connecticut. Printed in the United States of America by Vail-Ballou Press, Binghamton, New York.

Library of Congress Cataloging-in-Publication Data

Slavitt, David R., 1935–
    Virgil / David R. Slavitt.
      p.   cm. — (Hermes books)
    Includes bibliographical references and index.
    ISBN 0–300–05101–8 (cloth). — ISBN 0–300–05102–6 (paper)
    1. Virgil—Criticism and interpretation.   I. Title.
  PA6825.S57   1992
 ˙ 871′.01—dc20   91–13996

The paper in this book meets the guidelines for permanence and durability of the Committee on Production Guidelines for Book Longevity of the Council on Library Resources.

10   9   8   7   6   5   4   3   2   1

for Nina

ipsa tibi blandos fundent cunabula flores.
occidet et serpens, et falax herba veneni
occidet; Assyrium vulgo nascetur amomum.

CONTENTS

FOREWORD

"It would be a pity," said Nietzsche, "if the classics should speak to us less clearly because a million words stood in the way." His forebodings seem now to have been realized. A glance at the increasing girth of successive volumes of the standard journal of classical bibliography, *L'Année Philologique,* since World War II is enough to demonstrate the proliferation of writing on the subject in our time. Unfortunately, the vast majority of the studies listed will prove on inspection to be largely concerned with points of detail and composed by and for academic specialists in the field. Few are addressed to the literate but nonspecialist adult or to that equally important person, the intelligent but uninstructed beginning student; and of those few, very few indeed are the work of scholars of the first rank, equipped for their task not merely with raw classical erudition but also with style, taste, and literary judgment.

It is a strange situation. On one side stand the classical masters of Greece and Rome, those models of concision, elegance, and understanding of the human condition, who composed least of all for narrow technologists, most of all for the Common Reader (and, indeed, the Common Hearer). On the other side stands a sort of industrial complex, processing those masters into an annually growing output of technical articles and monographs. What is lacking, it seems, in our society as well as in our scholarship, is the kind of book that was supplied for earlier generations by such men as Richard Jebb

and Gilbert Murray in the intervals of their more technical researches—the kind of book that directed the general reader
not to the pyramid of secondary literature piled over the burial
places of the classical writers but to the living faces of the writers themselves, as perceived by a scholar-humanist with a
deep knowledge of, and love for, his subject. Not only for the
sake of the potential student of classics, but also for the sake
of the humanities as a whole, within and outside academe, it
seems that this gap in classical studies ought to be filled. The
Hermes series is a modest attempt to fill it.

We have sought men and women possessed of a rather
rare combination of qualities: a love for literature in other languages, extending into modern times; a vision that extends
beyond academe to contemporary life itself; and above all an
ability to express themselves in clear, lively, and graceful English, without polysyllabic language or parochial jargon. For
the aim of the series requires that they should communicate
to nonspecialist readers, authoritatively and vividly, their personal sense of why a given classical author's writings have
excited people for centuries and why they can continue to do
so. Some are classical scholars by profession, some are not;
each has lived long with the classics, and especially with the
author about whom he or she writes in this series.

The first, middle, and last goal of the Hermes series is to
guide the general reader to a dialogue with the classical masters rather than to acquaint him or her with the present state
of scholarly research. Thus our volumes contain few or no
footnotes; even within the texts, references to secondary literature are kept to a minimum. At the end of each volume,
however, is a short bibliography that includes recommended
English translations, and selected literary criticism, as well
as historical and (when appropriate) biographical studies.
Throughout, all quotations from the Greek or Latin texts are
given in English translation.

In these ways we hope to let the classics speak again, with a minimum of modern verbiage (as Nietzsche wished), to the widest possible audience of interested people.

John Herington

PREFACE

PUBLIUS VERGILIUS MARO WAS BORN AT ANDES, A VILLAGE NEAR
Mantua, on 15 October 70 B.C. . . .

But even to address such a subject as the thumbnail life
of the poet is to venture upon controversial ground. After all,
what has the poet's life to do with his work? A help in understanding some of the references, perhaps? Well, yes, but there
is a certain kind of scholarship that was questioned for a
while—historical criticism, it was called, by the new critics
and then the deconstructionists and textual analysts. And
now that deconstruction is under something of a cloud, these
old-fashioned methods are back in slightly updated clothing.
Their practitioners call themselves the new historicists now.

From outside the academy, we can relax a little and allow
that a certain amount of information is useful if not actually
essential. Gossip is generally delightful, and on occasion instructive. The temptation is to let the gossip take over entirely,
to reconstruct Lord Byron's checkbooks while ignoring his poetry. Biography is about people and is warm and attractive;
art, on the other hand, is rather more abstract and demanding—which is why the popular press loves to skip to the interview and tell us whether the author likes cats, drinks too
much, writes with a gold fountain pen, or lives in the middle
of the woods with his menagerie of semitamed fauna. For obvious reasons, the "People" section has always had a more
avid audience than the "Books" section in *Time*.

With Virgil, though, we can have it both ways. There is

a fairly detailed life by Suetonius, but it is fanciful and unreliable, so we can recite the information without taking it too seriously, eating our cake but having it too. Our intellectual purity won't be besmirched.

The name, first off. Vergilius is the Latin, from which "Vergil" would be the expected form and is the one many writers in English have used, more and more of them lately. "Virgil," however, is the legitimate English name and the one I like because it is slightly less pretentious. "Vergil" sounds to me just a little like the mannerism of those television anchorpersons who develop an instant and obviously fake Spanish accent whenever they have to pronounce "Nicaragua" and "Salvador."

But back to the life. Virgil was said not to have cried at his birth and to have had such a gentle expression as an infant as to give assurance of an unusually happy destiny. He spent his early life at Cremona, moved for a brief time to Mediolanum, and then to Rome. He was tall, dark, rustic-looking, suffered from stomach ailments, sore throat, headache, and nosebleeds. He was abstemious about food and drink, was homosexual and passionate for boys, especially Cebes and Alexander (whom he calls Alexis in *Eclogue* 2). He was rather shy and, in Naples where he had a country place, was called "Parthenias," which means "Virgin" or at least "Maiden." On his visits to Rome, he was said to have avoided admiring crowds that collected to follow him around, ducking into any nearby house, asking for refuge, and hiding there until the people outside went away.

After some juvenile work, he is said to have begun some large poem about Roman history which he abandoned. He then wrote the *Eclogues*, the *Georgics*, and the *Aeneid*, in three, seven, and twelve years respectively. His manner of composition from the *Georgics* onward was to dictate a large number of lines each morning to an amanuensis slave and then spend the rest of the day reducing them, in the manner of a she-bear licking her cubs into shape. The success of the *Eclogues* was

such as to make him instantly famous—at the age of thirty-one
—and win him the patronage of Maecenas for the *Georgics* and
of Augustus Caesar himself for the *Aeneid*, which was not quite
complete when, in his fifty-second year, Virgil died at Brindisi
on the eleventh day before the Kalends of October (21 Sep-
tember 19 B.C.) in the consulship of Gnaeus Sentius and Quin-
tus Lucretius. His ashes were taken to Naples and laid to rest
in a tomb two miles outside of the city on the via Puteolana.
His instructions had been that, at his death, his friend Varius
was to burn the *Aeneid*, but Varius refused to promise this. On
his deathbed, then, Virgil called for the manuscript boxes,
presumably intending to oversee their incineration himself,
but no one would bring them. (He left his executors instructions that they were not to publish anything he himself would
not have given to the world, but, at the "request" of Augustus, Varius decided to publish the *Aeneid* after all, making only
a few corrections and leaving the incomplete lines as they
were in his dead friend's text.

That Virgil is such an overpoweringly established writer
speaks against him as much as for him, as far as I'm concerned. It is a measure of my admiration for his work that I
can like it in spite of its being a Required Text of Western Civilization, and it is no accident that my real enthusiasms are for
the *Eclogues* and the *Georgics*. In fact, I have some real trouble
liking the *Aeneid*. I can admire it but I find it hard to warm up
to.

What I am hoping to suggest is that these poems of Virgil's are worth reading not because they are officially certified
Great Works of Art, but because they are humane, and
shrewd, and sad, and comforting. Because they really do
reward our attention and repay abundantly the effort they
demand.

Actually, I was first drawn to Virgil by Robert Graves's
nearly insane fulminations against him, remarks that were so
intemperate and insulting as to provoke my interest (an interest that had not, I confess, been much aroused at school).

I began, twenty years ago, reading and thinking about Virgil and translating some of the *Eclogues*. Eventually, I did all the *Eclogues* and the *Georgics* as well (these have recently been reissued). It was largely because of that book that I was invited to write this one.

Robert Frost used to say that his idea of a lively student was one who would duck assigned work to do something else of equal or greater intellectual challenge. My idea of a good book is one that you read in moments snatched between "assignments." This hasn't been the usual circumstance for Virgil, but times are changing, and a lot of the old requirements have been relaxed or abandoned. Whether his poetry is assigned or not, it remains true that Virgil's work is still worth reading, and I hope to have served one of the laudable aims of the Hermes series in demonstrating that.

Perhaps my main worry is that I have not been clear about the fact that these are poems, that there is a play of language and image, a physical kind of appeal which is the fundamental business of poetry. I never know how to explain that sensuous apprehension of language. Technical discussions of prosody are surely not the way to go about it. And here, where the text is in Latin, there are further and greater difficulties. If you know Latin well enough to read it, you may get some sense of its chewiness and orderliness. But if not? You have to trust me, taking what I say at least partly on faith. I have done the best I could, supplying, for the *Aeneid* at least, Robert Fitzgerald's splendid versions to which I invite the reader to attend in every possible way. Not just the meaning, but the music, the energy, the stress and *tristesse* of the lines as they dispose themselves on the page. For the *Eclogues* and the *Georgics*, I have used my own translations.

ACKNOWLEDGMENTS

Considerable portions of this book were written during residences at the Villa Serbelloni, the Rockefeller Foundation Bellagio Study Center, and the Northlake Foundation's Villa Djanouni. I am grateful to these institutions.

My thanks also go to John Herington, whose patience and good humor saw us through a lively series of discussions that have been of enormous benefit to me (which I hope is reflected in the book). Finally, I thank Penelope Laurans and Random House, for permission to quote from Robert Fitzgerald's splendid translation of the *Aeneid*; Harcourt Brace Jovanovich, for permission to quote from Sophocles' *Antigone*, translated by Dudley Fitts and Robert Fitzgerald; the University of Chicago Press, for permission to quote from Richmond Lattimore's translation of the *Iliad*; and Tony Harrison, for permission to cite lines from his poem "Study."

PART I
THE ECLOGUES

THE RULES OF THE GAME

IN THE MINDS OF MOST PEOPLE WHO ARE NOT SCHOLARS AND classicists, Virgil is the author of the *Aeneid*. Italo Calvino suggests in the opening of his wonderfully intelligent *If on a Winter's Night a Traveler* that there are "the Books You Needn't Read, the Books Made For Purposes Other Than Reading, Books Read Even Before You Open Them Since They Belong To The Category Of Books Read Before Being Written," as well as "Books That If You Had More Than One Life You Would Certainly Also Read But Unfortunately Your Days Are Numbered." It is regrettable but true that Virgil's other works, the *Eclogues* and the *Georgics*, fall far too frequently into that last category with people who are not to be despised. (At least they've heard of them.)

I shall begin with the *Eclogues* and the *Georgics*, and then move on to the *Aeneid*, which many people have read some of, which almost everyone has to some extent absorbed by osmosis even if without opening its pages, and which has, all too often, prevented an exploration of the earlier and, to me, more congenial works. With the *Aeneid*, about which I have mixed feelings, I shall do my best.

The *Eclogues* are as inviting and easy to like as the *Aeneid* is difficult. Their surface is immediately attractive and then, on further examination, they prove to be intelligent, even profound poems—which is more than we ought to expect in the work of a young man. And the Virgil of the *Eclogues* is obviously young, a bright, ambitious fellow looking to make a reputation for himself. He is on occasion, brash and nervy but, at the same time, disarming. The *Eclogues* (it means "Selec-

3

tions"), also called the *Bucolics* ("Country Poems"), are actually an artful, urbane, even citified set of performances which invoke the tradition of Theocritus, the Greek poet of the third century B.C., but do so mostly to play with it. This early work of Virgil's is, at least in part, manifesto poetry—poetry about poetry and the lit-biz and also about poetry's great subjects. The poems reach out, therefore, particularly the even-numbered ones, to address and include most of life.

There is an unabashed glitter to the *Eclogues* and, in Virgil's complicated reworking of the Theocritan precedents, an even brighter dazzle he achieves from the inevitable comparison the readers were invited to make between his work and the earlier, paler Greek poems, most of which mean more or less what they say. The interesting exception is Theocritus's *Idyll* 7, "Harvest Home," in which the poet offers himself dressed up as Simichidas, the goat-herd. Virgil adopts this strategy of disguise and pretense and extends it to contrive a similar but much more pervasive program of refraction and allusion. These shepherds of his are not intended to convince anyone of their authenticity. They come quite unabashedly not from real fields and meadows but from a kind of playground Marie Antoinette maintained at the Petit Trianon, dressing up as milkmaid or shepherdess. The transparency of the get-up was part of its point, because Virgil's subject was not at all country life but Rome—where the complications and pressures, the pace and sometimes the ennui of the city dwellers' sophisticated and competitive existence could make the lives of shepherds and farmers seem not only desirable but "real."

The machinery of the pastoral has sometimes been compared to the old joke about capturing an alligator with a telescope, a pair of tweezers, and a matchbox. The trick is to look at the alligator through the wrong end of the telescope so that he appears to be very small. Then, picking him up with the tweezers, one—very quickly!—pops him into the matchbox, shutting it tight. This is, of course, absurd, and yet it has a momentary plausibility and even an applicability to Virgil's practice in the *Eclogues*. The speed required to bring off the capture is crucial because, if the alligator realizes what is happening or if the hunter becomes self-conscious and remembers himself and his vulnerability, disaster is inevitable. So with the shepherds in the Virgilian poems. As long as we are quick about our business with them and don't question them or ourselves too closely, they can, at least briefly, pass for rustics. And what we are then able to capture turns out to be a not inconsiderable haul that Virgil puts into their mouths as the honest simple truths of country folk.

Actually, it isn't anything of the kind. But as long as he can persuade us, or as long as we conspire with him and grant that these are unsophisticated bumpkins, we are able to accept what they are saying as if it were the hard-won result of taciturn lives spent close to the soil—or, to put it more plainly, not the same damn chat we're sick of from the fifth Lucullan banquet we've had to endure this week.

What is the point, one may ask, of so elaborate a piece of rhetorical machinery? The uses Virgil puts it to, or finds for it, are richly various. To begin with, the slightly exquisite townsman is likely to have a notion—whether accurate or not is beside the point—of some better life, some simpler, truer, purer existence, that is available elsewhere, or that used to be possible in "the good old days" but is now lost, perhaps forever. That simpler life—of childhood, of the country, of Eden—is no more than a dream, a mere fantasy, but Virgil realized that it could be a useful fantasy, re-energizing the rustic figures he was offering and, through the reader's own dissatisfactions and longings, endowing them with a gravity and authority no young poet could manage were he to speak *in propria persona*. It is not at all incidental that from the dignity and authority of the earlier poetry—here, Theocritus's *Idylls*; later Hesiod and then Homer—Virgil draws a kind of legitimacy. His allusion to the earlier work is enough at least partially to disguise his impressive innovation. His Roman audiences were beguiled, lulled by the seeming conservatism of his reference, and therefore less wary than they otherwise might have been, so that Virgil was free to say whatever he liked and still expect his audiences not only to listen but to yield to him. To put it more concisely, Virgil had contrived a way of speaking that combined the interest of novelty with the authority of a "classic." A neat trick, then or now.

The transformation of Theocritus was an act of interpretive analysis by which Virgil first of all intuited not only the covert strategies of the Greek poet's work but the possibilities for extension and extrapolation of those strategies that Theocritus had not, himself, suspected. The earlier poet had understood how the appeal of country life is intensified for the urban audience. The indifferent landscape in the poems of Theocritus becomes a venue for innocent expression of simple emotions and, by implication, an emblem for innocence itself. Hesiod had written of a golden age that was past, and this is what Theocritus contrives to invoke. But even if he wrote as a man of the city, he was no stranger to country life and did not have to invent from whole cloth the pastoral figures of whom and through whom he spoke. For Virgil, however, the country was an almost purely imaginative construction. His countryside is virtually a dreamscape, a product of fantasy and yearning upon which no real shepherd has ever set the crude foot of actuality.

Thus, wholly untrammeled, Virgil can invest his pastoral figures with no more than a pretense of rusticity; the merest gesture is quite sufficient to identify a mode of thought and speech. As readers, we take our cues obediently enough and attend to the words as if they were in quotation marks. Or, to put it a slightly different way, the pastoral machinery is like the proscenium arch of a theater in which a modernist playwright is in residence. Sometimes he follows the convention and uses the arch in traditional ways but at other times he plays with it—or against it—working his effects by the violation of the stage's frame.

Eclogue 1 sets the tone—or, one might better say, the range of tones—for the entire series. Meliboeus and Tityrus are country folk, both more and less real than any whom we might have encountered in Theocritan Sicily. What they are talking about is politics and the implications in the hinterlands of decisions that may be taken in Rome. In a curious way, what Virgil starts with is not at all metaphorical but rather the literal basis for his flights. Decisions are made in Rome and men write words on wax tablets and papyrus—and their words do not merely describe but actually create the country. The goats, the houses, the very hills and meadows open or close, exist or do not exist according to the meanings of those words, deeds, and orders.

What Tityrus says about Rome, almost at the outset makes clear to us something of the disproportion between the countryside and the capital:

> The city they call Rome, Meliboeus, I used to think,
> Dope that I was, was just like ours, where we herd
> Our kids and lambs. I thought they grew up, as puppies
> Grow to be hounds. I had worked it out in my mind.
> But Rome is different, as cypresses, standing tall,
> Are different from the drooping shrubs around them.
>
> [1.19–25]

As the primacy of the government in Rome is awesome, an enormous and even god-like responsibility for the governors, so the poet's burden is also awesome, for he is creating these figures and their landscape with his pen as surely as are those officials in their state offices who register deeds and whose job it is to confiscate or not, evict or not, and who can favor the small landholder or destroy him.

What *Eclogue* 1 is about is power and, of course, its opposite, powerlessness. The two herdsmen, Meliboeus and Tityrus, are consoling one another, for while one has been displaced, the other has contrived some intercession from a connection in Rome. One is leaving and the other has ar-

ranged matters so he can stay—but they are both losers, and
each of them is sympathetic to the plight of the other.

The ordinary relation of the country to the city in the pastoral tradition as it came to Virgil was a degree of idealization
of the countryside. What Virgil does that is quite novel is to
turn the landscape real and, at least a little, to idealize the
characters. The decorum is stately, stoical, suave—everything
any Roman would hope to be, himself, in such a moment of
trial. These two friends exchange their stories—Meliboeus,
the one who has been displaced, and Tityrus, the other, who
has perhaps been humiliated, having at the very least discovered in the transaction in Rome (whatever it was) that he is
not the independent and autonomous person he's always
thought himself to be. Tityrus invites his friend Meliboeus to
remain at least for the night:

> This one night, you might have rested with me here
> On the green grass. We've got ripe apples, chestnuts,
> An abundance of pressed cheeses. Look at those
>   housetops
> With chimneys smoking, as the mountain shadows fall.
>   [1.79–83]

So? What does Meliboeus say? What is his answer to this generous, friendly, and perfectly reasonable invitation? Nothing!
He doesn't say a word. Instead, in the resonant silence that
follows Tityrus's last speech, Meliboeus just turns away, unable to accept, or perhaps unwilling to profit by, an indignity
he has not, himself, undergone. It is a grand and terrible moment.

The pastoral, Virgil here announces, is to be understood
from now on in a new way, with nature as a backdrop for
historical action. The notion of nature as timeless or, at most,
as an unchanging round of reliable seasons is false—as anyone who has actually lived in the country can testify. Indeed,
the whole idea of nature is here subject to a new and more
rigorous scrutiny. The usual conventions—or temptations—

are to think of nature as either much better than human character and action, imposition and exploitation—as in the famous line from Reginald Heber's "Missionary Hymn" about how "every prospect pleases, and only man is vile," or else to suppose the contrary and take the view that nature is dreadful, the dark place beyond the glow of civilization's firelight. This is the harsh world to which Tennyson alludes in his "In Memoriam," in which man

> trusted God was love indeed
> And love Creation's final law—
> Tho' Nature, red in tooth and claw
> With ravine, shrieked against his creed.

Either of these positions is a sentimental polarization, a distortion of the truth that Virgil seems to take for granted—that nature is indifferent, neither better nor worse than civilization, but only (or at most) different. His interests lie elsewhere, in the distinction between experience and intellection, or between reality and art. The pastoral figures on the page—or, on occasion, on the stage, for some of these poems evidently were performed, like Jacobean court masques—seemed to Virgil sufficiently interesting to engage as artistic constructions. Nature, when he refers to it, can be harsh, as it is to the kids that Meliboeus's goat bears on the flinty ground where they die, as the displaced herdsman tersely reports. But that severity is continuous with the larger obduracy of all the world's experience, the domain of raw fact we must all contrive one way or another to deal with, or anyway to suffer.

This incipit is no mere accident of composition but a deliberate decision on Virgil's part. *Eclogue* 2 is thought most probably to have been the first in order of composition. But the arrangement of poems in a book is a matter to which most poets are likely to pay some careful attention. The first and sometimes the last are the pieces likeliest to attract the attention of browsers. More important, and more to the point here,

Virgil was eager to establish landmarks as early as he could to let his audience know where to place him and how to attend to what he was saying. The departures from Theocritus are, in *Eclogue* 1, striking. In the second poem, it is the similarities and echoes we notice—to Theocritus's *Idylls* 3 and 11, both of which are complaints of unrequited lovers.

But even here, at the beginning of the undertaking (if, in fact, Virgil did begin here), there is a kind of extension that transforms the material. The desire Corydon feels for Alexis is not what we would think of as a grand passion—which is a later European invention. There is, indeed, a touch of comedy in Virgil's treatment of the lust Corydon himself realizes is hopeless: the figure he cuts is in part ludicrous, and Virgil holds his enraptured bumpkin up for more than a little ridicule. But he is not an utter clod. He lets us know:

> I have an instrument—seven hemlock stalks
> Of graded lengths went into its making: Damoetas
> Gave it me on his deathbed, long ago
> Saying, "You'll be its second and lucky slave."
>   [2.36–39]

This may or may not be another empty boast, but it is an interesting note for Corydon to sound, for if passion is sometimes absurd, we are all, from time to time, its victims. Or at the very least, we are its potential victims—which means that the passions are, like the politics that lurk outside the circle of the first *Eclogue*'s focus, one of the risks of living. The simple shepherd who can be displaced by the stroke of a distant pen is also vulnerable from closer threats—a saucy look, or a smile, or even a sneer. And frustrated ardor also has the advantage of being an occasion for song, as requited love or satisfied lust seldom have been.

Even at this point, we may perhaps begin to speculate about the direction of the collection—or of the single poem, if that is what it turns out to be. The contemporary fashion for the poem in parts, the suite, may enable us better to under-

stand the machinery of Virgil's debut piece. What Wallace Ste-
vens and Robert Penn Warren looked back to was a tradition
of which this is the primary source, for the earlier collections
of pastoral poetry—of Theocritus, Bion, and Moschus—were
just that, mere agglomerations of work. The *Eclogues*, however, can be read as a composition, their juxtapositions and
correspondences having occasioned a considerable amount of
scholarly and critical interpretation. Even at this early stage,
with only two dots to connect, we begin to see at least the
possibility of a line—a public displacement and a private de-
rangement, each of them being an occasion for song.

That architectural consideration is not simply another
question we have to keep in mind but a source of possible
enlightenment about the particular pieces, a way of understanding something of the function of each element, the stress
it is intended to bear, the weight of its meaning. And if there
is an internal eviction—from order, security, and even san-
ity—then it doesn't at all matter that the object of Corydon's
passion is treated in a slightly comic manner. It is, to begin
with, a homosexual passion—about which Virgil is not likely
to have been moralistic and condemning, but which he may
have assumed that his readers might regard with a degree of
detachment. It is, at the very least, a minority taste—which is
enough to make it, to the rest of us, slightly funny. It lacks
any justification of procreativity which heterosexuality can at
least theoretically claim, and is therefore slightly frivolous and
self-indulgent. One needn't go to any homophobic extreme to
be able to see Virgil's point—which is simply that there is no
accounting for the promptings of the passions. They seize
upon us and we in turn seize upon inappropriate objects.
Alexis may be handsome or even dishy (*formosum* is Virgil's
word) but he also happens to be his master's plaything, *delicias
domini*. There is, then, an urbanity about him, and at least a
possible suggestion that Corydon has not only picked the
wrong and hopeless quarry but that he is way out of his
league. Corydon is, after all, a country person, a simple shep-

herd who cannot expect to compete with the comforts and
diversions (and corruptions) of the town.

To make matters even worse, Corydon is no fool and realizes all this, or at the least he is able to describe the situation
in ways that make his plight clear to us:

> The fierce lioness chases the wolf; the wolf,
> The goat; the goat the clover's blossoms; and I
> Chase you, Alexis, as each is dragged along
> By his own particular fancy.
>
> [2.63–65]

It is a measure of his helplessness that he knows his pursuit
is vain and yet is unable to abandon it. His closing bit of advice
to himself is correct but useless, for it does no good to remember how one can always find another to chase after. That consideration is within the domain of reason, which is what he
has been evicted from. And his song is the signature of that
displacement.

This is no contrived modern reading, no textual trans-
mogrification in which the inescapable fact of the poem's
being a poem becomes arbitrarily the point of the exercise. In
fact, Virgil calls attention to Corydon's music making and puts
into Corydon's mouth the specific claim of having a set of
pipes Damoetas gave him long ago on his deathbed, with the
odd promise—or warning—that Corydon would become the
instrument's "second slave."

Not master we note, but slave, as Corydon is a slave to
his passions. The equivalence is striking. We remember how,
in *Eclogue* 1, Meliboeus addresses Tityrus in the very first line
of the work, as the latter lies on the ground, serenading the
woodland spirit with his reed pipe. That pipe is so obviously
a piece of the conventional pastoral costume that we may not
have taken any particular note of it. But Corydon's mastery/
slavery of the syrinx is another prompting. And to settle any
doubt that may remain, any possible reluctance we may still
have about reading the poem in this self-conscious way, *Ec-*

logue 3 settles the matter for us conclusively. This is a variation, or re-vision, of Theocritus's sixth, eighth, and ninth
Idylls, in which a variety of shepherds and cowherds hold
singing contests. In the sixth, Damoetas and Daphnis compete
and the judgment—Theocritus makes it himself—is that neither was the victor and that they had both won. In the eighth,
Daphnis and Menalcas compete and an unnamed goatherd
decides that Daphnis has won, leaving Menalcas "downcast,
his heart weighted with grief, like a virgin's when she is wed."
In the third of these competitions, the odd *Idyll* 9, the first-
person narrator is either Theocritus as himself or else in the
guise of the goatherd, and this narrator applauds both performances and says that his allegiance is not to either performer but to the art, to the Muse, herself. In Virgil's version,
the competitors are Damoetas and Menalcas, and there is a
third figure, Palaemon, a farmer who comes along and judges
the performances. There is no clear outcome, however. Palaemon likes them both, but in any event the fields he has
been irrigating look to be wet enough, and it's time to call it
a day. Which doesn't have an awful lot to do with art except
to suggest that in the real world, it is difficult to get the attention of the public and almost impossible to hold onto it. The
real world intrudes as represented by the farmer who has
practical concerns to deal with, is, at best, willing to listen but
not much involved, and therefore—let us not kid ourselves—
is not particularly knowledgeable, either. The curious relationship that obtains between the poet and his audience is
here—for this debut work is being done, or at least being published, in the hope of obtaining some sort of audience. Or patronage. Or both. There is no notion of any widely popular
attention—democracy is not one of Virgil's hobby horses, and
the idea of a democracy of taste would have seemed laughable
to him. But there is a need for a sponsor, a patron like Maecenas or, later, Augustus, to whom he could look for support
of various kinds (including, of course, material support). But
what does a patron really know? The proper judges of poetry

ought to be the ones who do know, which is to say other poets—but they are competitors, like Menalcas and Damoetas. Their judgments are skewed. As Auden has pointed out, poets are not the ideal readers of poetry because they tend to prefer the work from which they can learn (or steal) to work that may be superior but cannot teach them anything. And that disability leaves the job to those who are not qualified and not very much interested—like Palaemon, a man with fields to irrigate and other, harder, rows to hoe.

(There are literary critics, of course, but that is a relatively modern job description. The classical literary critics—Aristotle, Philodemus, and the others—were philosophers interested in describing a curious phenomenon, a special kind of reality that might enlighten other aspects of experience. The modern critic—the kind who distinguishes good from bad, or who presumes to lecture not only to the general reader but to other critics and even the authors themselves—stands in the narrower heritage of Dr. Johnson, who discovered that there was a living to be made [not necessarily a rich one, but still a living] in instructing recent arrivals into the middle class how to spell and how to think about [and, more important, how to talk about] poems and plays. With these aides, the arrivistes were on their way, could issue correctly spelled dinner party invitations to their friends, could conduct themselves properly at table [the dictionary and etiquette book come from this same period and are clearly related], and then, during the meal, could talk acceptably and correctly about plays and other literary works. Then, after the event, they could write one another orthographically correct letters of thanks. None of this has much to do with the working poet or playwright or novelist. Indeed, except insofar as these tastemakers have an influence on the kind of living he makes, the grants he gets or fails to get, or the academic appointment he can wangle, the whole business of criticism is entirely alien, as the complicated life of the anthill is alien to the aphids the colony may keep as if they were dairy cows.)

For the purpose of the pastoral, the audience is Palaemon, who is better than none at all. At least he is willing to
stop what he's doing and listen to the two poets. And if his
judgment is not dispositive in this eclogue, that isn't so bad
an outcome. There is, in *Eclogue 7*, a winner, and there the
subject is what winning means or doesn't mean, and how success and failure can be arbitrary and unfair. But before Virgil
can consider the capricious results of the relationship that exists between creators and consumers of literary artifacts, he
introduces the relationship itself and its inevitable imperfec-
tions.

By their natures, artists are interested in art and suppose
it to be central to the human experience. Most people, who
are not artists, would take a quite different view of the matter
and think of art (if they think of it at all) as an embellishment
to life, a sprig of watercress to pretty up the platter but not,
in itself, a source of nourishment. It is not our object here to
assess the relative truth of these different views. What is to
the point is that Virgil's basic assumption (we may suppose)
is that art is of value. He is, after all, engaged in the making
of it. The contrary view—which is what I believe he would be
drawn to—is the one he introduces here, and it is a view that
is of interest only in a highly urbane, refined, estheticized setting. To say that art is bunk, or is irrelevant, or is of only minor
importance is not to say anything important or noteworthy in
some pioneer outpost where the overwhelming question is
one of survival. But in a sophisticated cityscape, where one
has been living for some days almost entirely on the canapés
and cheap white wine of gallery openings, that kind of suggestion takes on a different weight. We need at such moments
to be reminded that people's need for air, water, food, clothing, and shelter is somewhat more pressing than their need
for reading matter.

The Greek idea that only a man of leisure was a full man
was an extraordinary insight. One who devotes every bit of
his time and effort to staying alive in a simple vegetative way

is, in some sense, a vegetable. To be a complete person, one must be free of those obligations so that there is at least some opportunity for the pursuit of beauty and truth (art and philosophy). Well, sure, that's true. But it is Virgil's understanding in the *Georgics* that the man of absolute leisure has no connection to what we think of as "the real world." The gruff uncle who asks, "Has he ever met a payroll?" may be lacking somewhat in refinement, but he is not wholly wrong. And Virgil's flirtation with the life of the soil represents at the same time a proclamation of urbanity and a declaration of urbanity's limits. The fun little farm one keeps in Connecticut for weekend visits is exotic and interesting only to the people who would not otherwise find occasion ever to get out of the east sixties. That *nostalgie de la boue* is Virgil's invention—to which I shall of course be returning later. I mention it here as a way of explaining how what I take to be the usual Virgilian contrariness informs these eclogues' statement about the artist's real relation to his reader.

Virgil is not delighted with Palaemon, but he is perfectly well aware that the man did stop, listen, and at least allow the two singers to take up some of his time as they performed. And that is about all the performer has a right to expect. The performances themselves are not particularly compelling, and it would therefore be easy to misinterpret them, which is what happens if we take them straight. What redeems them, turning them from one kind of poetry into another, is nothing in the world but the quotation marks Virgil puts around these effusions. We are like the audience in *Der Rosenkavalier* when the Italian tenor does his number in the first act, listening to him of course, but hearing him at least in part across the distance on which Strauss and Hofmannsthal relied. It is an attractive enough song, but it is also a joke, the composer's way of making fun of a different tradition of operatic composition. There is no such parodic intent in the lines Virgil gives his competitors in *Eclogue 3*, but their turns are very conventional, even stylized, performances, and I believe that we are supposed to attend to them in that particular light. To put it another way, it would be unjust to read these passages as lyric poetry, although that is what they look like; the better way is to look at these lines as dramatic, which takes nothing away from their lyric aspects but also frames them so that they are at once less and more than what we would see if we were to take them as naked exercises in antiphonal versification on traditional themes.

MATTERS OF LIFE AND DEATH

The ordinary categories of literary discourse are inadequate here. *Eclogue* 4 is an exercise in exaggerated compliment to celebrate the birth of a child in the year of Pollio's consulship (40 B.C.). Taking the occasion of this birth and extrapolating from it to the revival of hope that comes—or ought to come—with the birth of any baby, Virgil describes a utopian existence in which the earth will yield up its crops without the arduous labor of farmers and in which sheep will come in all colors so that people won't have to dye wool any more. This, he says, is the baby who may get us out of the mess we're in, whose appearance may mark the dawn of the new age.

It is an elaborate, fairly mannered piece of writing, and it has a certain charm. Its relation to the real world is minimal, almost perfunctory, but there is a connection. We might compare this eclogue to the *carpe diem* poems like Marvell's "To His Coy Mistress," which are at the same time ridiculous and also serious. Their argument is that we're going to die so we might as well go to bed together, and the suggestion is at once perfectly absurd but also true (because sex is, among other things, the species' way to triumph over the death of the individual). In that same generalized way, Virgil's exaggerations have an undeniable ring of plausibility to them, and the poem works and evokes in us not only admiration for its flight of fancy but also an acknowledgment that there is something earnest and honest in its hope. The tension is between hope and skepticism, and the balance shifts, if only a little, when a new life begins.

That's it. And that's enough—or it ought to be. But *Eclogue* 4 is also Virgil's ticket to fame. This is what the Christians seized on, claimed for their own, and used to claim Virgil himself as a prophet of the coming of Christ. A baby will come to get us all out of this mess? Close enough! And the utopian world in which there is no more plowing and in which there is no need for sailors to risk the perils of the sea . . . it's near enough to Eden, isn't it? One could push it only a little and see it as evidence of a Messianic visitation. So Virgil gets to be a kind of pre-Christian Christian, almost a saint (he was, until fairly recently, actually mentioned in the Mantuan liturgy).

This is not a reading to which I am drawn. It seems not only absurd and wrong-headed—this couldn't possibly have been Virgil's intention—but unnecessary, because the poem is perfectly explicable in nonsupernatural terms. Still, while one can argue with literature and literary theory, it is impossible to argue with history, and the historical fact is that much of Virgil's success over the millennia has depended upon the coincidence of this poem's conceit and the importance of the Nativity in the Christian religion. Whatever the place Virgil had in the classical curriculum, he managed to maintain his position and even to improve it by impressing the monks in the Middle Ages. The monasteries were the spore cases, preserving the germs of Western learning, and it was Virgil's luck at least to get himself copied out more often than might otherwise have happened because of the aura of sanctity, that nimbus if not actual halo he owed to this piece of writing.

Outrageous! And, of course, also correct—for these poems are in part about literary reputations, the arbitrariness of fame and fortune, and misfortune, and the ways in which we must learn to endure their extremities. Donne's poem about the lovers that uses a compass is still intelligible and powerful—as it would not be if he had chosen, for some reason, to work up a conceit based on the astrolabe. There is a randomness to these things, an utter irrationality which, if we concede it, allows us to assume a posture of at least some degree of detachment and amusement. There is the tough literary agent whom a writer I know reports as having once said, "Art is for kids; this is a business!" That's true, but not yet the whole truth. There are consequences of success or failure, prosperity or want, and any artist knows moments when he or she finds it hard to resist at least a little envy at the improbable and unaccountable thriving of a colleague. Virgil's *Eclogues* begin with that kind of admission—a courageous thing in any poet, and all the more remarkable in a young one.

In a weird way, then, the random association that got made between the birth of Jesus and this fourth *Eclogue* that Virgil wrote some forty years earlier is a kind of pay-off in what was always a literary sweepstakes and remains a mostly aleatory business. That Virgil wrote in Latin rather than Aramaic or Egyptian was lucky for him. That Christianity came along to make a fetish of this particular poem was, in the same way, a piece of good luck by which he might have been amused, and which he therefore deserved as much as anyone can deserve one of these gifts that floats down from the sky.

Or, to look at it in quite another way, we might decide that there is something appropriate in the way the world has given Virgil particular credit for having hit upon one of the great Christian themes. Whether or not we accept the religion and believe in its dogmas, we must acknowledge its success and allow that it has contrived a way of speaking to the great emotional and spiritual needs of mankind. There are excesses perhaps, encrustations that have been added to the original impulse, but there is a truth in the simple and unadorned form of the story. The infant Jesus is affecting because he is like all infants. Wordsworth was embroidering on the Christian tradition when, in "Intimations of Immortality," he wrote that "trailing clouds of glory do we come / From God, who is our home: / Heaven lies about us in our infancy!" There was no such tradition for Virgil to rely on. He had to invent it, starting with the primitive emotions any of us must feel when looking down into a cradle and seeing the helpless baby just starting life. It can be a complicated business, a mixture of pity and envy as we think of our own lives and compare our hopes with what we have actually accomplished. We consider this child, as yet unblemished by disappointment or disfigured by dishonor, and we are struck by the terrible coming down that inevitably awaits him or her.

Or is it inevitable? The strength of the Christian nativity story is just what Virgil prefigured in this eclogue—as he makes the suggestion that there may one day be a child whose course is not inevitably downward but who somehow soars upward and is therefore the hope of the rest of us. What he imagines is not the terrible career of a Christ but the paradise to which we will be returned, that lost Golden Age for which each of us mourns, blessed or cursed by some dim memory of the bliss of childhood—which is, of course, the other connection we tend to make of infancy and paradise. Freud might see it as the grief we feel for the exchange we made of the freedom of the body for what we call civilization. And perhaps it is—fundamentally—a question of toilet training. To have to control one's own body, to have to accept delays and wait to eat or go to the bathroom is to come down in the world from the lordliness of the infant, who does what he wants whenever he wants, and whose helplessness is a kind of awesome power.

There are many such myths of an earlier and better age that crop up in a range of cultures and societies, and Virgil here invokes that dream of a better life of which the innocent infant is a representative and for the recovery of which he also holds out some hope. What the Christians pounced upon with particular glee was his coda in which he says what he would have to say on such an occasion:

Behold, the world with its vaulted weight bows down,
And the lands of earth and the tracts of the sea, and see

How everything in the age to come rejoices.
If only the last days of a long life could remain to me,
And enough breath, I shall sing of your great deeds,
Nor shall anyone excel me in singing, not Orpheus,
Not Linus, even if he had the help of his mother, Calliope.

[4.50–56]

It is not necessary to interpret this to mean that he is expecting
to live those four decades to attend the birth of Christ in a
remote part of the empire. It is a sufficient explanation to say
only that he acknowledges here that he is, at the birth of this
baby, a grown man. If the baby does do something wonderful
thirty years from now, if the extravagant predictions of the
poem are in some way fulfilled, Virgil will by then be old, if
he has survived at all.

But what are these boasts about, anyway? The claim is
that from the deeds of the newborn child the poet will draw
special powers and that his celebration of the marvelous heroic exploits will earn him fame and even immortality. It is a
bit odd, perhaps, but it seems to the modern sensibility no
more than another extravagance, similar to but congruent
with the earlier rhetorical conceits and exaggerations that have
been the building blocks of the poem. It needs to be pointed
out, then, that this last suggestion represents a radical shift,
even an absolute reversal of the Homeric idea of the relation
that obtains between the hero and the bard. In Homer, the
poetry is the instrument by which the hero and his deeds arrive at their immortality. The poet is like a priest of the hero's
cult, keeping alive the memory of the great man's accomplishments. Here, in Virgil, the hero is the primary figure and the
poet rides into immortality—if he does so at all—hanging on
the hero's coattails.

This is, in part, another tactful expression of praise for the
life that will be lived by the new arrival. It also suggests a more
modest, more realistic and tough-minded attitude about the
literary profession, in which some element of luck is assumed,

as well as the truth of the proposition that poets need heroes
more than the heroes need poets. And Virgil's luck was, as
usual, at least as great as his talent (and both, clearly, were
monumental). There have been attempts to speculate about
what baby might have been the intended recipient of these
extravagant compliments, although none of them seems very
satisfactory. But then, perhaps their unsatisfactoriness is the
issue. Possibly it was Mark Antony's child Virgil had in mind,
but Antony lost and Octavian won. Octavian, on the other
hand, had only daughters (or, if you follow the line down a
few generations, you can get to Nero, who seems hardly to fit
Virgil's bill of specifications). You would perhaps allow for a
female child of Octavian, but in that case the baby turns out
to be Julia—whose main accomplishment may have been getting Ovid banished to Tomis for his tangential complicity in
her flagrant sexual adventures (perhaps he may have lent her
his apartment).

That there is no Roman baby of the year of Pollio's consulship whom any sane person could, in retrospect, identify
as the likely child, the hope of the nation and the world, only
underscores our rueful longing for such a deliverer. Enmired
as we are in wickedness, corruption, and infirmity, we require
innocence and purity to save us. Looking down into a cradle,
who does not think inevitably of the innocence he once had
and has now lost? We see a baby smile and the hardness of
our hearts mollifies as we smile back with some all but forgotten fragment of that original blessed blamelessness we
can still recognize in ourselves, and we are surprised and
ashamed.

> Begin, little boy: Smile and know your mother.
> In her tenth month now, she has suffered long pains
>   for you.
> Begin, young man. Smile for the folks, or you'll never
> Dine with a god or take some goddess to bed.
>
> [4.60–63]

The fifth *Eclogue* is a kind of answer to the fourth, or one might better call it an inversion, for if the fourth considers nativity, the fifth is concerned with death. Or no, it's not that clear cut. There are two shepherds, Mopsus and Menalcas, who are involved in another of those singing contests of the kind we have already seen in *Eclogue* 3. This time, the subject of their songs turns out to be the death of Daphnis, or more generally death itself—which is not surprising. Mortality is one of the great mysteries, and therefore has always been one of the great subjects for poets.

What must strike us as being at least slightly irregular is the distance Virgil puts between this death and us. It isn't a pressing grief, really, that moves the poets. These two figures are performers, Mopsus a specialist on the reed pipe and Menalcas a singer. And they cast about for a suitable subject for their friendly competition. Menalcas makes other suggestions—the passions of Phyllis, the praises of Alcon, or the Quarrels of Codrus—and it is only then that Mopsus begins his dirge. So there is no possible question about the death being, primarily, an occasion for art, which is at least the co-equal subject here. Indeed, the better and clearer view of this poem is to consider it as an examination of the encounter between the two domains, a consideration of the powers and limitations of art in the face of death. The drama, then, is one in which the antagonists turn out to be eloquence and silence.

The dirges the two rustics perform make sense only if we understand that they are addressing these specific questions of how a literary artifact may serve to keep someone who is dead alive in memory. This radical transformation that is possible through art is one from mortality to immortality—and therefore from humanity to divinity. Mopsus begins by declaring—rather flatly, almost reportorially—that "the nymphs mourned Daphnis destroyed by cruel death." The question to which Mopsus and Virgil then turn their attention, and direct ours, is what good that expression of grief may have done to

Daphnis, what difference it may have made—or what difference it ever makes.

They sing, performing their dirges, both of which are exaggerations of grief—which tends to exaggerate itself anyway.
In that of Mopsus, Carthaginian lions roar their grief and the
hills and woods give voice to their sadness. But Menalcas's
answer—partly a topper, partly a conclusion—is to push
Daphnis just a little further and turn him into a god, dress him
in white, and set him at heaven's gate.

The notion of the poet as the one who enshrines the hero
and through whose song there can come a kind of immortality
is not a new one. The Greeks believed this more or less literally—as Gregory Nagy argues in *The Best of the Achaeans*. For
Virgil, however, the idea is old, lifeless, tattered almost to a
cliché in which nobody really believes. But Virgil's extraordinary strategy is to accept this lifelessness and play on it—
which is why the exaggerations in the two dirges are so stylized and conventional.

The real question, then, turns out to be whether Mopsus
and Menalcas can persuade one another, or can even bring
themselves again to believe in the magic of poetry. That it was
once in the power of the poet to immortalize is now almost
forgotten, and that memory is nothing to be proud of but, on
the contrary, almost an affront. The poets may or may not do
anything to keep Daphnis's memory alive, but it turns out that
by their performances they are able to comfort one another.
And if that has happened, their efforts have not been entirely
inutile.

Virgil assumes that something has happened. The important dramatic verses of the eclogue are those which Menalcas says to Mopsus at the end of the latter's song:

> Divine poet, your song is to us as sleep
> To the weary man, exhausted, on the grass,
> Or as cold spring water to one who is parched in
> the heat. . . .

By this time, we have come to realize that it is a spiritual exhaustion of which Menalcas speaks and a metaphysical thirst. Menalcas will join Mopsus in the attempt to carry Daphnis "to the stars," or, in plain terms, to make him one of the immortals.

The end of the poem is a Theocritan exchange of gifts and compliments, almost rueful, for neither of the shepherds supposes that their attempts have been successful. Daphnis is still dead, after all. Nothing appears to have changed. And yet, if we allow Daphnis to have represented, in some sense, some dead Roman, and if we imagine Mopsus and Menalcas as Virgil's peers, poets he knew and perhaps admired, poets for whom the magic of the craft was sometimes more than their faith could encompass—then we have to see them as in some sense successful, even triumphant. Two millennia have passed, and we are still reading their dirges for their dead friend, which is an astonishing circumstance. The putting of word with word, foot with foot, and line with line has indeed managed the astounding transformation the old poets propounded as a part of their purpose.

Virgil is suggesting that we have to think of the poet's craft in more ambitious terms and understand that the art is not simply another genre, one more form of entertainment among the many on offer. Neither is it a specialized if often pretentious branch of rhetoric. There is a continuum that may start at one end with lyrics to beer-drinking songs, dirty limericks, children's riddles and jingles, but it extends to the loftier heights of epics and hymns, and to assert one aspect is not necessarily to deny any of the others. For a young man's manifesto work, to include the grandest claims of poetry is a dangerous gesture. To make such an attempt and to fail would be profoundly embarrassing. But in a strategy that is clever in its modesty and tactfulness, Virgil has his two poets perform, has them seem to think of their performances as failures, has them exchange their compliments and gifts almost as consolation prizes—and then he allows us to realize what they may not have understood themselves, which is that they haven't failed.

And that too, sad as it may be to contemplate, is a correct representation of how it often is with poets and their work. They can succeed and neither know it nor take from it the pride and joy they have earned.

A BRIEF RESPITE

If the range of poetry is from epics and hymns to drinking songs, then, to be complete, this young man's declaration of rights in the domain of poetry must extend to include the drinking song. And even though this is, for Virgil, something of a reach, he contrives an elaborate carom shot to get where he wants to go. He may not be able to present himself as any kind of lounge lizard or barroom brawler, but he can invoke the god of drink and, from the abstract idea of drunkenness, descend to the specific and suggestive details of his otherwise awkward subject.

The first dozen lines of *Eclogue* 6 that establish the frame of the poem are an extraordinary example of rhetorical inventiveness. What Virgil is devising here, and what Ovid exploits later in the *Tristia* and the *Epistulae ex Ponto*, is a poetry that depends for its effectiveness on how we perceive it and whether we understand it to be direct statement or dramatic posturing. We are required to determine what is in quotation marks and what isn't. In Ovid's poems of exile, the tension is precisely there, in those quotation marks—which give way from time to time. The pretense of sniveling and toadying, which is so exaggerated as to be obviously an artifice, every now and then collapses as Ovid seems to drop the mask and let us perceive his own face, which is—of course—also contorted with grief. In dramatic climaxes, the feigned grief often turns real—or as real as anything in a poem can be (outpourings of real grief do not usually express themselves in elegiac couplets).

Ovid's master, I have always thought, was Virgil, whose

practice in the *Eclogues* amounts to a kind of fan dance in which, from time to time, we can see through the feathers of poesis to a "real" poet on stage, performing and even teasing us with glimpses of some further mystery or "truth." At the outset of this eclogue, we have Apollo advising the speaker, Tityrus, that he was wrong to have abandoned the *légèreté* of pastoral verse in order to celebrate in a weightier way the military exploits of his friend Varus. In conformity to this command of the god, then, Tityrus announces to Varus—to whom the poem is addressed—that he will again take up the reed pipe but dedicate the work to him.

It is a cat's-cradle of complication. Apollo is always Apollo, but is Tityrus a mask for Virgil? Is he the same Tityrus we met in *Eclogue* 1, the one whose farm was saved by intercession from someone in Rome? Well, maybe. (Suetonius tells us that Virgil actually did write about military exploits, or at least he attempted some such project, perhaps on the subject of Alba Longa, the early settlement of the Trojan survivors in Italy, but gave up, only to return to epic poetry later on.) Is Varus the Publius Alfenus Varus whom Servius identifies as having been a fellow student with Virgil under Siro the Epicurean—and who was later appointed as one of the commissioners to allot lands to veterans in northern Italy? Possibly, possibly.

The point of this little proem seems to be an apology that Tityrus will not be celebrating Varus's exploits after all, but instead will be dedicating this poem to him. This is a bizarre beginning which only makes sense later, as we come to the introduction of Gallus—who is hardly a pastoral figure. Here the mask drops and instead of Tityrus we get the actual Virgil talking *in propria persona* about his famous, ruinous, and eventually ruined friend.

We may think of these violations of the conceit as the weights to the rhetorical balloon, the proofs without which its buoyancy could hardly be demonstrated. The balloon, itself, is the appearance—and celebration—of Silenus, the drunken

god. Young Chromis and Mnysallus discover the god asleep,
perhaps stuporous, his garlands askew, and, with the aid of
Aegle the Naiad, they tie him up, refusing to let him loose
until he makes good on his old promise to sing for them. It is
a prank, a piece of buffoonery, until Silenus sings. And then:

> And then you might have seen the Fauns and the animals
> Dance to his tune, and stodgy oak trees nod.
> What Apollo's music does for hard Parnassus,
> What Orpheus's songs accomplished, moving Ismarus
> And Rhodope, Silenus was able to match.
>
> [6.27–30]

This is not what we anticipated. The drunken god is
roused and one expects him to sing something about five hundred bottles of beer on the wall. But the subject of his song is
creation, nothing less. The majesty of Lucretius is what we
have here: the coming together of earth, air, fire, and water
to condense into a globe; the hardening of the land and the
separation of the waters; the effects of the sun's rays in evap-
orating water to make clouds; the coming of the life-giving
rains so that the woods begin to grow and the beasts appear;
and then, finally, the arrival of man.

What has any of this to do with Silenus? Or with drink?
The connection is so clear that Virgil doesn't even bother to
make it, but leaves it to us to realize that there is often an
irrational element to creation and that, along with Apollo, Di-
onysus has his place. Creation is too serious and risky a business to be limited to the powers of light; the dark powers—of
the unconscious or even of drunken inspiration—have their
dignity, must play their part, and must be given their share
of credit for whatever is in the world.

Silenus sings of some other myths. Pyrrha's throwing of
stones to make men may be a part of the creation legend. He
mentions the reign of Saturn, tells the story of Hylas, and then
offers a peculiar version of Atalanta's story (it neglects to mention her name). This omission and the lack of orderly transi-

tions among these pieces suggest that Silenus may not yet be quite sober, even if he is awake. Then, to conclude, Silenus gives us details of the life of Gallus—which come not from Silenus or even "Tityrus," but clearly from Virgil himself.

Gallus is Gaius Cornelius Gallus, a remarkable man who was Virgil's friend and fellow poet. With Varus, Gallus was a commissioner for the redistribution of lands in northern Italy; he was also the author of four books of love poems and was one of the foremost Roman elegists. Both Propertius and Ovid wrote admiringly of his work.

But Gallus was a poet as Walter Ralegh was a poet, splendid but by the bye, during moments when he was not occupied as a soldier and statesman—and it was these latter occupations to which he increasingly gave his energies. He was one of Octavian's trusted lieutenants and he served him for many years with distinction. Gallus held a high command under Octavian at the battle of Actium in 31 B.C. and was entrusted with the pursuit of Antony to Egypt. Dio Cassius praises him as a resourceful and imaginative military commander. After the death of Antony, Gallus was made first prefect, which is to say he was more or less the governor general of Egypt, and it was in this capacity that he put down a rebellion at Thebes. But as E. V. Rieu puts it, "Power had gone to his head and affected his judgment. Instead of attributing his successes to the Emperor, as tact and policy demanded, he claimed the merit for himself, had his own statues erected everywhere, and even caused self-laudatory inscriptions to be put on the Pyramids. He had enemies enough to ensure that such conduct should be reported at Rome and interpreted as evidence of disloyalty. The matter was dealt with in the Senate, Gallus was recalled, and, though not condemned to death by his old friend Augustus, felt that he had fallen beyond redemption and took his own life" (*Virgil: The Pastoral Poems*).

Well, this is all very interesting, but it takes a moment or two to make the connection. What has this to do with Silenus and his song of creation? We assume there must be some relevance somewhere and that, under the guise of the god's semi-inebriated rambling, Virgil is clear-headedly contriving some significant gesture. The convention of the man of action—the military figure or, in the last century, the big-game hunter—off in the rough in order to find some distraction from his romantic wound, is an extreme case, but there is something of that idea here. Gallus is famous as a love poet, writing elegiac verse to Lycoris. He suddenly stops this and devotes himself instead to the service of Octavian—and one may make the leap from *post hoc* to *propter hoc,* supposing that in the strenuousness of warfare and government service out in the provinces, Gallus was trying to forget the woman who had caused him some anguish.

We may, if we choose, think back to Corydon, in *Eclogue* 2, but here the point that Virgil is careful to make is that Gallus was crazy. Virgil is not eager to antagonize Augustus, after all, but neither does he want to speak ill of his friend. Later on, after the disgrace of Gallus, it will be impossible to advert to him at all, and Virgil will have to revise the ending of the last book of the *Georgics* to substitute something else for what we are told was another passage about Gallus. But to use him here as an example of the kind of madness that knows no bounds and is not responsible . . . is to be at once sympathetic to Gallus and yet regretful of what has befallen the man.

Virgil will return to the subject of Gallus's downfall in *Eclogue* 10. Here, he doesn't do more than allude to Gallus who, wandering in the wood, is presented by Linus, Apollo's son, with a reed-pipe. . . . Gallus's talent is no protection against what is going to happen to him, nor is the disorder of his life or the inebriation of love any impediment to his singing. Or to the singing of Silenus, as a matter of fact. Silenus may be a little blurry, but "his music rang in the valleys and the valleys echoed it up to the stars." The evening star rises and the two reluctant young men, Chromis and Mnasyllus, tear themselves away to drive their sheep home for the evening count.

There are still problems. It is not absolutely clear why Vir-

gil should be dedicating this celebration of Gallus—an apo-
theosis, almost—to Varus. What was the relationship among
these three? Were the two men friends? Or all three? School-
mates, perhaps? Servius reports (although he is not always to
be believed) that Virgil's recitations of this eclogue so im-
pressed his friends that he was moved to have it staged, and
it was performed by Cytheris—the woman Gallus had loved
and addressed in his poetry as Lycoris. Which surely was no
mere coincidence. It is diverting to suppose that the relation-
ships among the three men were similarly intricate and that
Virgil might have been getting some extra-textual glide from
those extrinsic associations. Although the timing is most im-
plausible, Servius maintains that Cicero reports himself to
have been "stupefactus" at these performances of the eclogue
by Cytheris, and even if this didn't actually happen, there may
have been some such element of gossipy interest in the work.

   If the drinking song in *Eclogue* 6 turns into a more serious
business about chaos and creation, the friendly competition
between two poets in *Eclogue* 7 also has a twist to it. This is
another of these amoebaean challenge dances, but with a couple of differences. One is that each round is four lines rather
than two, which is hardly earth-shaking. The other, more important innovation is that here, there is a winner. Corydon
triumphs. And, obviously, Thyrsis loses—because if there is
a winner there must also be a loser.
   This seems to be a not very complicated representation in
pastoral terms of what happens in the real world in the lit biz.
There are winners and losers. One tries to suppose that, in
the long run, some kind of rough equity prevails, but that is
an imposition of more or less willful blindness. Why should
writer A prosper and writer B—every bit as good as A—lan-
guish? It is unfair, of course, and not what we might have
preferred, but that's how it is. Which doesn't mean that there
aren't people to argue the contrary case. Even here, where
there is not much difference between Corydon and Thyrsis,

there are wrong-headed if right-thinking commentators like
Prof. H. J. Rose (see *The Eclogues of Vergil*, 1942) laboring to
find defects and blemishes in Thyrsis's style.

But Rose is missing the point, which is that there are no
significant differences and that luck has a good deal to do with
success and failure. Luck and maybe character. It is possible
but probably not significant to distinguish between the characters and personalities of Thyrsis and Corydon, but such considerations ought to be beside the point. In any event, Virgil
has found a way to fudge things just a little. We don't see the
contest in an unmediated way. There is a narrator, Meliboeus,
who reports the proceedings, and at a certain point his memory fails him:

> That's all I remember. Thyrsis tried and lost.
> From then, it was Corydon. All the way.
>   [7.69–70]

One would suppose that to be clear enough. It isn't even
claimed that Corydon "won," whatever that means. But it is
Thyrsis who loses. And his defeat leaves Corydon the victory
almost by default. Which is one of the ways it happens in the
world. One way to succeed as a writer is not to drink yourself
to death, or go crazy, or die in a plane crash.

But even that isn't always reliable. I remember once discussing this tetchy subject with an older writer, and I told
him—I was younger and more brash then—that it wasn't so
deep a mystery. All you have to do, I said, is stand in line long
enough, and the awards and prizes and the recognition will
eventually come.

"You think?" he asked, staring into his drink. "Look at
Wright Morris! A fine writer. But consider his career." He took
a sip and then looked up at me to explain, "You stand in line
long enough, and they'll move the fucking store!"

It is in that grim tone that I read those last two lines of
Eclogue 7. "From then, it was Corydon. All the way."

Eclogue 8 gives us another pair of shepherds, Damon and Alphesiboeus, but there is no competition here. One sings and then the other sings, in an informal way, or perhaps in a comradely exchange of the kind we saw in *Eclogue* 5. Their subject is love and its complications, or at least that is the ostensible topic of their singing, for what emerges eventually is a special view of love and its relation to poetry. Art can be a consequence of pain, but it can also be a cure, not necessarily reliable or effective but no more bizarre than the incantations of Damon's song and the magic spells of which Alphesiboeus sings. Poetry is, itself, a kind of magic—either in its pure state or, as here, in the fellowship of art.

It may not be that two poets are better than one, but in each other's presence they are perhaps better able to believe in what they're doing, or to resist their own doubts and fight their moments of despair. The world is usually inhospitable to an art that demands so much and seems to give so little. But at moments of anguish, we are all driven back to fundamental and even primitive resources of the spirit, and as any religion demonstrates with the hymns and chants of the various liturgies, song is one of these.

It seems to me that this is Virgil's claim here and the real subject of this apparently simple but actually fairly complicated little poem. That there is a fellowship of talent seems a necessary qualification of the statement of *Eclogue* 7. It is true that there can be rivals, enmities, and jealousies between and among poets. There are often iniquities of talents and of their rewards. But there can also be a reinforcement that comes from the companionship of the two performers, their shared understanding and the similarity of their trials giving their association an importance that two farmers or shepherds or merchants wouldn't need and therefore couldn't imagine.

The eclogue begins with a kind of dedication, almost certainly to Pollio (to whom *Eclogue* 4 is also addressed), a soldier and in 40 B.C. a consul but also a poet who wrote tragedies that are lost but were praised by Virgil and by Horace as well

(*Odes* 2.1). The witchcraft is conventional and comes largely from Theocritus, but here its use is metaphorical, the shepherd's magic standing for the subtler magic of poetry. Damon sings first, leaning against the trunk of an olive tree. He calls upon the morning star and complains about Nysa, whom he has loved but who has married Mopsus. Damon is miserable, complains that the gods haven't helped him, haven't heard his prayers or listened to his vows, and he declares that he will soon be dead. The refrain to this, which he repeats throughout his performance, is another kind of prayer, not to love or to the gods but to the Maenalian reed pipe (Maenalus is the mountain range in Arcadia sacred to Pan). He asks the pipe to accompany him and to play with and for him as he goes on about how faithless Nysa is, how cruel Love is, and how senseless life without Nysa and Love now seems:

> Now let the wolf flee in fear from the lamb;
> Let oaks bear golden apples; let narcissus
> Bloom upon alder bushes; let amber sweat
> From the tamarisk bark; and let the screech-owls sing
> Better than swans.
>
> [8.51–54]

The short version is that there is no logic left in the world, that the basics have given way and, in a kind of spiritual free-fall, Damon is in a state of despair. His plan is to go up to a windy cliff and leap to his death into the sea below, making his death into a spiteful wedding gift for Nysa.

Alphesiboeus answers, but his reply has nothing directly to do with Damon's anguish. He is singing instead of Amaryllis and Daphnis, and he has Amaryllis casting spells to bring the errant Daphnis home. What this does, of course, is to take everything that has gone before and put it into quotation marks. Damon is no longer personally aggrieved or grieving but now only has an authorial connection to the persona of his song: there is no necessary identification of any particular traits or troubles as his own. If, in the second song,

Alphesiboeus isn't Amaryllis, then Damon isn't limited or defined either by any suffering of the voice of the first song.

This is already a magic as impressive as any that Alphesiboeus describes, although those descriptions are interesting,
intentionally quaint pieces of folklore that had the same back-
country associations then that they do now. There are effigies,
pieces of the indifferent lover's clothing, magic spells and
symbolic sacrifices. And then, surprisingly, the result is that
they are effective:

> See how the flames dance on the altar. The ashes
> Stir on their own before I touch them. It works!
> Something is happening. Bowser is barking. It's real!
> Dare I believe it? Am I dreaming again? But no. . . .
>
> [8.104–07]

And the refrain, which we've learned to expect—"Bring him
home from town, my song, bring Daphnis!"—changes now,
and we get, instead, "Hush, my song. He's come back from
town. It's Daphnis."

Do we believe that the spells actually summoned Daphnis? No, probably not. But something else has happened.
Grief, Damon's actual wretchedness, has turned into something different, has been transformed into art by a kind of
magic more complicated and just as impressive as the sum-
moning by Amaryllis of her lover. In that case, Alphesiboeus
has responded properly and generously to his friend Damon's
expression of woe.

A RETURN AND A FAREWELL

The conceit of the pastoral is like any other conceit: it goes on
only for so long and then gives way. One of the charms of
soap bubbles is that they are momentary, and there are artifacts that take on a dramatic poignancy because they partake
of this kind of ephemerality. Our suspension of disbelief can
go only so far and then we begin to wonder. Maybe we even

look at our watches or check to see how many pages are left
on the right-hand side of the volume.

Virgil is perhaps conscious of this inner drama, for the
scale of the *Eclogues* seems calculated. I can think of no other
poetic work this short that includes so much and resonates so
long. In *Eclogue* 9, Virgil is already signaling the beginning of
a coda, for there is a return here to the not-quite-pastoral setting of *Eclogue* 1. We are still out there in the land of shepherds
but just barely, for there are seizures of farms which are violations not only of the security and independence of the farmers but also of the art form. Politics has no business in the
Theocritan pastoral; for Virgil, the interesting countryside is
that which a city dweller imagines—a fictive world which can
never be expropriated.

There are other violations of the pastoral conventions.
The two herdsmen meet, complain about their sorry plight,
and exchange tags of poetry—as a kind of consolation, or to
suggest in yet another way that the internal landscape is the
alternate arena to which one may have, in moments of trib-
ulation, recourse. But along with these snatches of songs and
poems they exchange are references to actual people—Varus,
for instance, to whom their friend Menalcas has made an appeal, albeit an unsuccessful one. Varus is the real Varus, in
which case it has been suggested that Menalcas might be Virgil—except that Menalcas in one of these snatches addresses
a Tityrus, and in *Eclogue* 6 Virgil had made it fairly clear that
the Tityrus mask was his own. There are also real poets from
Rome who come in for praise, Varius and Cinna, whom
Moeris praises. Cinna was a friend of Catullus. Varius was a
friend of Virgil's who served as his literary executor.

These may be appealing problems for graduate students
to chew over, but they are not seriously interesting. It seems
clear enough that the collapse of the pastoral conceit is part of
the intention. This and *Eclogue* 10, in which Virgil bids a heart-
breaking farewell to the form, may be taken together. The
complaints, then, of the herdsmen's displacement take on a

characteristic Virgilian doubleness: the loss of their farms is
real enough, too real even for traditional pastoral poetry; but
it also represents the exhaustion of the conceit, in which we
as readers are necessarily involved. (That involvement refers
back to the other literal loss, of course, and makes us more
sensible of the farmers' plight, but Virgil figured on that.)

And in the face of these literal and figurative losses, what
is there to do? The two herdsmen exchange snatches of poetry, or they do this as well as they can, complaining of their
losses here, too:

> Time sweeps all things away—even memory goes.
> As a boy, I would sing daylong till the sun went down
> Songs I knew by heart. But the heart can fail,
> As my voice is failing me too.
>
> [9.51–54]

Lycidas tries to cheer him up a little, but Moeris isn't buying
it. He has given it up. There is business to attend to. He says
that they can sing when Menalcas gets there, an ambiguous
suggestion that can mean either a) that we can sing Menalcas's
songs better when he is here himself, or b) that when he gets
back from his failed attempt, we can all console one another.

We get the choice, depending on our mood, our view of
the world, and our view of Virgil. My own preference—or
guess about Virgil's preference—is for the latter and darker.

Eclogue 10 begins:

> This is the last one, Arethusa. Help me.
> A little poem for my friend Gallus (and who
> Would refuse him that?) and maybe Lycoris too.
> Arethusa, begin, and may your waters flow
> Under Sicilian seas untainted with salt.
> Begin, and let us speak of Gallus' turbulent
> Love, while the she-goats graze on the tender shoots.
>
> [10.1–7]

It actually is the last poem in the series, and the effect is striking enough for Milton to have copied in *Lycidas*, the beginning
of which strikes the same note of woeful valediction:

> Yet once more, O ye laurels, and once more
> Ye myrtles brown, with ivy never sere,
> I come to pluck your berries harsh and crude,
> And with forced fingers rude,
> Shatter your leaves before the mellowing year.

Milton's purpose is to let us know that he is perfectly aware
that he is attempting to revive an apparently exhausted form,
but he is also referring, I think, to the opening of *Eclogue* 10
and its melancholy air of cloture. The conventions of the pastoral are strained by what seems to be the poet's negligence:
he doesn't even remember to hold the mask up to his face,
give himself some name out of the repertory's choice, and pre-
tend to be some kind of shepherd, nor does he use any pastoral name for his friend. He refers to Gallus directly, as he
has already done in *Eclogue* 6. (There, however, the direct reference was a rupture of an already established pastoral mise-
en-scène and it came quite late in the poem; here Gallus is the
subject, and, at the beginning of the poem, there is no set of
established conventions to violate.) There is, of course, an invocation to Arethusa, but this is a complicated piece of business Virgil has going. Arethusa tried to escape the pursuing
river god, Alpheus, and she was turned into a fountain which
flowed under the Ionian Sea and reappeared as a spring on
the island of Ortygia, on the Sicilian coast at Syracuse. It is an
odd story, but what Virgil means by it is that the source of the
pastoral (Sicily) is to flow beneath the sea and emerge to in-
spire Virgil at his writing table on the mainland of Italy—and
the waters of her stream ought not be mixed with the salt of
sea-brine or, for that matter, the similar salt of tears.

Then, in the seventh line, we get the goats as a kind of
afterthought, where Virgil remembers that he is more or less
committed to these pastoral conventions. But it is almost too

much for him to bother with them. After all, how much can
poetry do to soothe the grief a man feels for his friend's hard-
ships? It is a dramatic opening, and the dramatization of the
strength of Virgil's feelings is in the near collapse of the pastoral tradition to which he is bidding farewell here.

Gallus was well known to the Roman audiences, both as
a poet and as a soldier and politician. (He was, later on, a
spectacular failure—overstepping himself and earning the
disfavor of Augustus, so that he was obliged to commit suicide. But this ultimate disaster comes some years after the
composition of the *Eclogues*.) Gallus's fame made Virgil's
poem a more interesting and more daring violation of the conventions of the pastoral. The poetry—Gallus's poetry, that
is—had not been able to provide any solace. It was, Virgil
maintains, to try to forget his hurt that he had gone off to court
danger and the hard life. He is the poet *maudit*, the romantic
hero (millennia before romanticism), the poet for whom mere
literature is not sufficient. Gallus will go to find in the dangers
of the battlefield and the rigors of travel and adventure some
grander *poesis*, and an anesthesia, if not an actual cure:

> Tree nymphs no longer please me. Never mind
> Nymphs, the trees themselves have blurred
> To brown boredom, sticks stuck in the dirt.
> Wilderness is tame. I've seen the blind
> Snowstorms of Macedon, been in absurd
> Swelter of deserts, frozen, baked the hurt,
> But have it still.
>
> [10.62–69]

Then, addressing the Muses, Virgil suggests that these
lines must suffice. This is more or less what Gallus might have
sung. He does not say so, but we are not prevented from
thinking that his grief for Gallus has silenced him. It is either
this grief or the failure of his belief in poetry itself. And, indeed, Virgil says,

Let's go. This shade is bad for poetry.
It's juniper, sour. Nothing can grow in this shade.
And he herds his goats home. They've had their fill.

[10.75–77]

It is an extraordinary moment, eloquent for what it says,
more eloquent and moving for what it does not say. Inviting
us as it does to supply the missing information and to collab-
orate, it recruits us and makes us its partisans. The suspension
is not of disbelief but of ordinary critical resistance, because
we tend not to be critical of our own emotions and their expression, which is exactly the tricky feat Virgil has contrived
and the most powerful kind of communication there can be
between an author and his reader.

The collapsing conceit is a startling idea. Art is supposed
to be eternal, isn't it? "Life is short, and art is long," as Hip-
pocrates said. (On the other hand, George Garrett, the novelist and poet, has glossed the dictum, writing, "Art is long,
but I am short.") What Virgil is saying, it seems to me, is that
for all of poetry's attractive richness, one can't live there. The
pastoral world is the world of art, an abstract kind of world
that yearns for an elemental and natural opposite. The shades
of Hades need blood before they have enough corporeality to
allow them to speak, Homer shows us, and these artifactual
pastoral figures, likewise, want substance. Their country setting and their flocks of greedy goats ought to provide that substance, but of course they don't. The trees turn all too quickly
into stagehands' props, as the hillsides reveal themselves to
be crudely painted flats.

The drama is not just on the stage, however, but in the
auditorium, and in our own hearts, where we are torn between our sophisticated pleasures and the ennui or even disgust that can come of too much sophistication. There must be,
we think, a clearer, truer way to live, an existence in which
there are no more tiresome questions about what to order

from the menu and the wine list or where to go after dinner. Somewhere there are lives in which these questions never arise, in which there is no need for the exhausting self-aware- ness we have to put on early each morning before we decide what else to wear. We yearn for simplicity and necessity, and those are things the pastoral setting seems to offer.

Paradoxically, though, there is another, contrary mean- ing, for the pastoral figures are artifacts and stand, therefore, for the world of intellectual and artistic achievement, a world more remote but also more reliable than the contingent uni- verse in which we find ourselves. But it isn't Eden or heaven. Or, if it is, our belief in it fails, as it often fails, too, of Eden and heaven. Art is not a religion, however much we should like it to be, and it can't save anyone—surely not Gallus, and not Virgil either.

Well, what can?

Freud suggested that love and work were the two criteria of a tolerable existence. Love, as we have seen, is a risky busi- ness, but work is a sensible, sober idea. And it is to that, to the exploration of the demands and rewards of labor, that Vir- gil turned his attention in his next and greatest poem, the *Georgics*.

PART II
THE GEORGICS

THE IDEA OF COUNTRY LIFE

T. S. ELIOT'S ESSAY ON VIRGIL IN *ON POETRY AND POETS,* AL-though quirky and distorted, does offer at least one interesting and useful notion—the centrality of the *Georgics* to Virgil's thought and poetic achievement:

> It was the Greeks who taught us the dignity of leisure; it is from them that we inherit the perception that the highest life is the life of contemplation. But this respect for leisure, with the Greeks, was accompanied by a contempt for the banausic occupations. Virgil perceived that agriculture is fundamental to civilization, and he affirmed the dignity of manual labour. When the Christian monastic orders came into being, the contemplative life and the life of manual labour were first conjoined. These were no longer occupations for different classes of people, the one noble, the other inferior and suitable only for slaves or almost slaves. . . . Christianity did establish the principle that action and contemplation, labour and prayer, are both essential to the life of the complete man. It is possible that the insight of Virgil was recognized by monks who read his works in their religious houses.

Eliot's batty attempt to turn Virgil into a proto-Christian is not interesting to me. What I do find intriguing, however, is his suggestion of the Roman corollary to the old Greek notion of the primacy of leisure. If the Greeks realized that freedom and a degree of leisure were preconditions to anything worth calling human existence, the decadent sophisticates of

45

Rome came to see that a life of uninterrupted leisure was frivolous and hollow. These were the people who could think of
their home estates and the work of agriculture with a romantic, almost Tolstoyan nostalgia. Farming, for Virgil, is almost
an exotic thing to consider. He is the city dweller who looks
to the weekend place as a way to get in touch with "reality."
This is not so much an actual love of farming that we are
seeing as the dislike of urban life, the fatigue with fashion that
wants permanence, and the ennui that craves something truer
than the artificiality of politics and art, and chat about these
things. What I took to be the motive force of the *Eclogues* seems
to be operating in the *Georgics* as well, with more disgust,
more fervor, and an even greater yearning. The poet still uses
the agricultural landscape in a figurative way, but he takes
more particular notice of it now than he did in the *Eclogues*,
where specificity and consistency were generally ignored. (As
L. P. Wilkinson has observed, there are oxen drawing home
the plows at line 66 of *Eclogue* 2, even though Thestylis was
making a salad for reapers back in line 10.)

I agree with Eliot about the centrality of the *Georgics*, but
I think we read the *Georgics* rather differently. I see in the
poem a contrariety that goes beyond ambiguity to a bizarre
endorsement of the very opposite of what he seems to be af-
firming. The *Georgics'* celebration of the pleasures of farming
is feigned for literary and social reasons, just as the *Eclogues*
are in a certain sense a put-on. This back-to-the-earth poem
turns out to be quite bookish. Virgil is supposed to have had
an estate near Naples where, presumably, there were farm
workers outside, tilling the earth and tending the vines on the
property. He seems never to have consulted them, however,
but instead to have looked to his library, poring through Hesiod, Lucretius, and other writers for the literary precedents
he wanted. Literary precedence is interesting in a way that
scratching in the dirt just isn't.

There is also a tradition that there was a practical reason
for the poem, and that the idea was for Virgil to write some-

thing to remind his readers of the pleasures and rewards of country living—so that people might leave Rome, relieving its overcrowding, and return to the farms. Augustus's government may have had such a policy, and Maecenas may even have proposed some such propagandistic undertaking to Virgil, but even at the furthest limits of politeness and civility, Virgil would have done well to restrain himself and not burst out in derisive guffaws. What a sublimely stupid idea!

And yet, in some stupid ideas there can be a certain poignant charm. One returns to them, first to laugh and then, feeling sorry for them, to discover perverse ways of improving upon them, sometimes by turning them into jokes. Having been propositioned in this way, Virgil might well have decided that the ideal response was to admit its absurdity but then to have the last laugh by undertaking actually to do the poem, the very foolishness of which could be one of its greatest charms. It isn't essential to look at the *Georgics* this way, but it does them no harm. Imagine some professional writer who, offered the job of writing an owner's manual for Yamaha motorcycles, comes up with something like *Zen and the Art of Motorcycle Maintenance*. The conversion of the modest assignment into an occasion for a more ambitious and elevated project can be a source of triumph to a writer who recognizes that, for the most part, his activities are marginal and dependent.

That the *Georgics* pretends to be a didactic poem has scared off a fair number of readers, even though they have John Dryden's assurance that this is "the best poem of the best poet." This is not an extravagant claim or a demonstration of provocative wit by a poet but, I believe, a perfectly plausible judgment, one that Adam Parry more or less echoes when he writes that "the *Georgics* may well contain the finest expression of Virgil's poetic art," and declares it to be "one of the finest poems of all antiquity." Sure, sure, the modern reader thinks, shaking his head, but a two-thousand-line poem about farming?

The instructional quality of the poem is only a framework, an occasion for what is, ultimately, a series of descriptions and observations that operate musically, for the most part. The poem is a marvel of shifting tonalities and textures, an almost abstract composition that hangs on the didactic frame but seems virtually irrelevant to any discussion of farming. But there is, of course, a connection, for the poem's subject, it seems to me, is not agriculture but labor, any labor, and the redemption that is possible through the achievement of excellence. The work of the stockmen and the plowmen, the vintners and the apiculturists is metonymic for any kind of work. And the redemption that is possible through work is the one Virgil achieves through the labor of art, turning so unpromising and even silly an assignment into a triumph, and managing to encompass not only the arduous existence of the farmers but arduousness itself, which is a way to describe all of existence. This is, then, a work of art about work, and Virgil plays with these notions, exploring their meanings and implications and testing their limits. The opposite of work is magic, that wave of the hand by which impossible feats may be at once accomplished. But even with magic, there is a skill, a necessary art if the magic is to work—and book 4 ends in the story of Aristaeus (which is, itself, an *epyllion* or miniature epic), an account of the regeneration of the bee swarm from the rotting carcass of a young bull, and then the retelling of the story of Orpheus and Eurydice, which is another consideration of the possibilities of art in the struggle against oblivion and death.

Freud suggested that the two criteria by which one might judge whether a life was functional or not were love and work. If you can engage and cope in these domains, you are probably fundamentally healthy, and if not, then not. Poets seem always to have been yammering about love, which may "come along" and transform a dreary and uninteresting existence into something grand and rich. The surer way to find some meaning and richness in life, though, is through work, which doesn't depend on anyone else, and which is likely to determine, as much or more than the vagaries of our domestic relations, who and what we are. In *Eclogue* 10, Virgil wrote what must be his most famous line (69): "Omnia vincit Amor: et nos cedamus Amori" (Love conquers everything, and let us yield ourselves to Love). Early on, in *Georgic* 1, there is the less well known version (lines 145–46): "labor omnia vincit / improbus" (hard labor overcomes everything). Oddly enough, though, there aren't very many poems about work.

That farming is more Virgil's pretext than actual subject is clear from the discrepancies, which cannot be accidental, between what the poem describes and what was happening on farms all over Italy in Virgil's time. The account of the agribusiness in Varro's *De re rustica* of the same decade as the *Georgics* tells us that the effort to break up the latifundia and reestablish small holdings of individual yeomen had failed for a variety of reasons. There were economies of scale that made the small holdings inefficient; except for the mountainous regions of the far north, the geography of the peninsula was more suitable for the grazing of large flocks and herds; and the overseas military successes of Rome meant that the importation of cereals was cheap and secure (some seven million bushels of grain a year were imported to Rome). These successes, moreover, produced a class of wealthy capitalists who could afford to buy up small farms and consolidate them into larger and more profitable holdings.

This is not altogether unrecognizable today, when the survival of the family farm is an issue to which magazine editors call our attention every so often. (And they are often more deeply concerned about the survival of independence and autonomy than of the actual farms on which those abstractions are thought to flourish: the farm, in this semifantasy, is not merely a locus for the cultivation of crops and the raising of cattle but the seedbed of morality and character.)

In Varro's time and in Virgil's, the work of farms was

mostly done by slaves, and even the bailiff (*vilicus*) was likely
to be one of these. There is no reference in the *Georgics* to
slaves, however, and hardly a hint of any of these other less
than inspiring economic realities in Virgil's descriptions. He
writes, instead, of a nearly symbolic life on the farm where
the relation of the cultivator to his field and its yield is immediate and direct, and where he does his own work with his
own hands (*ipse manu salsasque ferat*, as in 3.394). Virgil's concerns are not limited to those Romans who might have been
planning to invest in agricultural holdings. His subject, which
is wider and grander, is how any of us can contrive to live,
how we can make our lives bearable, and how we can find
among our griefs and burdens some sense of meaning and
purpose.

There is a dark quality to the *Georgics* which is one of the
poem's most appealing characteristics. Virgil is a somber sort
of poet, one whom I take to be struggling with depression
most of the time. One of the ways of doing this, of course, is
to bury oneself in work, which is what Virgil may have been
doing here. The labor of the composition of the poem enters
into the work, for the poet calls attention to himself in a number of ways. For one thing, he is in the poem himself, addressing Maecenas, his patron. For another, the use of literary
precedents and his allusions to other works—a Virgilian habit
throughout his career—is more various and complicated here
than in the *Eclogues* or the *Aeneid*. The *Georgics* is probably the
most literary work of all classical poetry. The effect of what
we would now call its "intertextuality" must have been startling then; it is striking even today. To get some idea of what
the effect of this allusiveness must have been on Virgil's readers back then, we must remember our own first encounters
with "The Waste Land" or *The Cantos* and recall our awe, by
which I mean both our admiration and our fear. (Do people
really carry all that stuff around in their heads, we asked ourselves? And we wondered if we were expected to know all

this by heart, so that it resonates in our heads the way Eliot
was claiming it resonated in his?)

The work of the poem is the work of the poem's construction and composition. It is also the works of the poem, its machinery and those other works of earlier authors whom Virgil
revivifies, in part as a demonstration of how a work of art can
be something to fling into oblivion's maw, a better means than
the Orpheus story might suggest of keeping the artist alive.
There are passages that recall Hesiod's *Works and Days* and his
Theogony, and Lucretius's *De rerum natura*, but there are also
borrowings and transformations from Homer in the Aristaeus
episode, from the *Phaenomena* of Aratus, and from other writers such as Callimachus, Pindar, and Nicander of Colophon—
so that the fairly widespread nineteenth-century view of Virgil
was that he was a poet of limited originality and imagination.

It isn't that those nineteenth-century critics and scholars
were stupid or insensitive, though. One must make the same
allowances for them as we have learned to make for biologists
who, for centuries, were unable to guess what the function of
the heart might be—until someone invented a pump that op-
erated with valves, and then the physicians immediately realized that that's what a heart is. The kind of allusion that Eliot
and Pound made commonplace in modern poetry wasn't in
fashion in the nineteenth century. Now that many poets operate this way, it is possible to see how allusion worked in the
classical poets and to distinguish differences among them. For
some, literary reference was merely a game, an exercise in
which the poet could show off or challenge the reader to figure
out what the source was of the image or the line. Virgil could
engage in this kind of play which is, fundamentally, an exercise of a kind of wit, but his allusions could also be part of
a more serious undertaking. In Virgil, and particularly in the
Georgics, where the subject of the poem is the confrontation
of labor and art with death and oblivion, there is often an in-
tegral function to the literary references, each of which is nec-

essarily an extension and revivification of some earlier poet's work. In the trivial practice of salon poetry, Virgil has found a way of getting intellectual and emotional resonance, contriving a leverage from some of these references that would have seemed startling and impressive in the first quarter of the twentieth century.

The most useful way to consider the structure of the poem is, as I have already suggested, to think of it as a musical composition. There are thematic suggestions that are introduced, allowed to run for a while, dropped, then returned to, and often in their reappearance they are enlarged or modified. There are also the kinds of alternations of pace and tone that one might expect in music. (One doesn't want to go too far with this, though. The poem is in four books, which suggests the structure of a symphony, and a number of critics have seized upon this coincidence. Brooks Otis has gone so far as to designate the four books as *allegro maestoso, scherzo, adagio,* and *allegro vivace.*)

The scholarly attempts to analyze the construction of the poem are mostly interesting for their unsuccess and irrelevance. These are scholars and analysts, after all, and they believe in intellection, so they are trying to discover principles and rules by which the poem hangs together. Even if such principles could be deduced, they would be useful only in the construction of a poem exactly like this one—for which, as long as we have this one, there is no earthly need. German philologists are particularly fond of this kind of exercise, and their analyses, which begin sensibly enough, enumerate the main techniques on which Virgil relies. (K. Witte notes [1] paralepsis, or putting subjects aside for later discussion; [2] repetition of words or thoughts; and [3] the use of counterpart passages.) But they get lost in elaborate mathematical computations of numbers of lines, as if there were some formula on which Virgil relied rather than the more real if more frail sense of how the poem felt to him, and what it seems to call for at any given juncture. (G. E. Duckworth's *Structural Patterns and Proportions in Vergil's "Aeneid"* is a curious attempt to demonstrate how the Golden Section explains the shape and structure of the entire poem.)

It isn't something critics and scholars want to hear, but the truth of the matter is that the composition of poetry is as much a physical as a mental undertaking. The Housman test for good poetry—whether it made his hairs prickle at the back of his neck—is something literature professors make fun of, because it makes them uncomfortable (or even guilty, if they've never felt it), but it's as good a test as any. Auden's way of judging a poem was to copy it out in long hand, and whenever his pen hesitated, he looked to see if there was anything wrong—and, more often than not, found something.

What one needs in the face of such a poem is modesty. Whatever we may infer about the construction of the *Georgics* is likely to be provisional and approximate. We must expect subtlety and be supple enough to be able to deal with that. The poem is a marvel that defies all our reasonable expectations, like a chocolate soufflé which ought to be too heavy to rise but which, as we can see, has risen nevertheless. What gives *The Rape of the Lock* its glossy finish is that while Pope is making a joke and writing a mock-epic, there is a gravity to the poem, more than a hint of *profondeur*. Conversely, there is an element of game playing in Virgil's mock-didactic poem that distracts us some from the bedrock of his melancholy. Or better, say that the strategy is to let the melancholy grow upon us, taking us at least partly unawares.

The *Georgics* opens with a triple invocation; to Maecenas, Virgil's patron; to the constellations and the gods who govern the seasons and the yields of farmers' labor; and then, twenty-five lines in, to Augustus Caesar. Virgil sets out the program of his four books, announcing that he will be discussing crop management, viticulture, animal husbandry, and apiculture. After the proem, he turns to the subject of field crops and how different kinds of soil and varying situations will produce dif-

ferent results. What he is doing here is mostly establishing his
authority and a tone of voice.

But then, in the 125th line, we get an intrusion of a different kind of material. It doesn't strike us as out of keeping
with what has gone before—Virgil is trying to make it look
like just another piece of rumination—but it is the first place
where we get some hint of what is really going on:

> Before Jove's time, no farmer subdued the fields
> Nor was it lawful to mark out boundary lines
> On the open plain. People strove in common,
> And the earth, herself, freely produced all things,
> Even before they'd been asked.
>
> [1.125–28]

It's the myth of the Saturnian golden age, that prelapsarian paradise in which there was no need for labor and art. And
the purpose of Jove's plan in putting the poison into the ser-
pent's fang, in stirring up wolves as predators and the tur-
bulent seas is

> So that by cerebration we might put
> Experience to work, excogitate arts
> To coax the wheat from the furrows and strike the sparks
> Buried in the flint's heart.
>
> [1.133–35]

Low on the list of what farmers need as they set out in the
morning for their work in the fields is a theodicy. The usual
explanation of this passage is like that of L. P. Wilkinson, who
says that this justification of the ways of the gods to men is
"not merely giving relief from didactic precepts, but providing
thus early in the poem a religious and philosophical mainspring which affects it through and through." Well, yes and
no. It is always delicate and even dangerous to try to separate
a poem's factual *donnée* from its flights of intellect and fancy
in order to consider the relation of the two kinds of writing.
In Louis Martz's study of the English metaphysical poets, he

made a useful observation of the derivation of the pattern for many of John Donne's and George Herbert's poems in the meditations of St. Francis de Sales. There was a tripartite structure to the poems that came, he maintained, directly out of the tradition of religious meditation: a composition of place, which was the ostensible subject of the poem; an exercise of understanding, which was the middle part, the intellectual complication or the guts of the poem; and the exercise of will or judgment, which was the inspiring coda, usually bringing the speaker into a new and more harmonious relationship either with the Creator or with His creation.

There are few instances, however, of poets working with so clearly articulated a set of specifications, and Virgil had no such intellectual template but was making it up as he went along. It seems to me misleading, if not actually presumptuous, to suppose, simply on the basis of what the title is and what the poem is pretending to be, that the agricultural information is in some way primary while such divagations as the theodicy are secondary, either "relief" or internal machinery ("a religious-philosophical mainspring"). It is at least as likely that the agricultural material is pretext and that the point is the expressions of Virgil's bedrock belief in the arduousness of existence and the precariousness of any achievement or even respite. That struggle for survival the gods have imposed upon us is perhaps responsible for our skills and accomplishments, but no amount of effort or cunning can protect any of us from the caprices of nature. The first book ends with a consideration of the signs of the weather to which farmers look for guidance and then, more generally, the apocalyptic warnings of the heavenly bodies of such cataclysmic events as the Roman civil wars.

What is required is that we read in an open, receptive way, letting ourselves be led, paying attention not only to the poem but to our own responses, which have, after all, been manipulated and programmed by the poet. That the expository material about agriculture doesn't necessarily seem like pretext and that it is convincing on its face only demonstrates Virgil's impressive proficiency. The magician's left hand is busy with flourishes and passes, and while our attention is thus distracted, the right hand is busy with the production of the gold coin, or the endless handkerchief, or the live pigeon.

The theme of *Georgic* 1 is the miserable human condition, that we are forced to labor and that our labor doesn't save us or protect us from death and oblivion. Book 2 is rather more cheerful, about trees and vines. Book 3, ostensibly about animal husbandry, discusses the raising of livestock, who as animals are subject to passion, which leads to annihilation and tragedy. Book 4 is the conclusion of the poem, a resolution of its contrarieties with a melancholy suggestion about collective survival and the perdurability of art.

A farmer may not find much of this directly helpful to the management of his fields and barns, but if he is interested in knowing what it means to be a man, to be a human being, then this is his poem. Work is what we are, and it is by our work that we assert and defend ourselves, if only temporarily, against the chaos and emptiness of the universe. Remembering his days in Auschwitz, Primo Levi wrote in *The Drowned and the Saved* that "work could . . . at times become a defense, as it was for the few who in the Lager were made to exercise their own trade: tailors, cobblers, carpenters, blacksmiths, bricklayers. Such people, resuming their customary activity, recovered at the same time, to some extent, their human dignity. But it was this also for many others: an exercise of the mind, an escape from the thought of death, a way of living from day to day. In any case it is common experience that daily cares, even though painful or irksome, help take one's mind off more serious but more distant threats."

Virgil understood this, and it is the remarkable achievement of the *Georgics* to keep both the pains and the rewards of labor and also those more distant threats clearly in view, and to suggest how there can be a balance, however ephemeral, between them. That balance is what we may term the human condition, and it is a truer and more humane representation of it, I think, than what we see in the *Aeneid*.

The epic we read in part (and in parts) out of obligation. The *Georgics*, however, we read in admiration and gratitude.

A HARD ROW TO HOE

The second book of the *Georgics* is the happiest of the four, having to do largely with viticulture and arboriculture, both of which presuppose an act of faith. To put in any ordinary crop, a farmer is required to believe that he will be left in peace for a growing season. Vines and trees take even longer and require therefore an even greater degree of reliance on the benevolence of man, nature, and the gods. One plants trees thinking not only of one's own immediate return on the investment but of the yield that will come to future generations:

> A tree that springs up from some random seed will grow
> Slowly, giving its shade to your descendants.
>
> [2.57–58]

Cultivation, a word that we use as a synonym for civilization, is primarily the cultivation of fields. The metaphoric force has been almost lost, but Virgil sees it fresh and vivid. The first book has just ended with its striking image of the farmer plowing the Macedonian plain at Philippi, turning the earth and exposing a helmet or white bones of soldiers. This book commences with a celebration of the virtues of the olive that can send out fresh shoots from cut, dry wood, and of the possibilities of grafting so that the stock of a plum tree can be made to produce cherries. In the production of olives and wine grapes, and in the variations in the woodlands of different regions, Virgil sees an opportunity for his most sanguine view of country life.

The descriptions here seem closest to actual didactic poetry, but their aim is not so much instructive as diversionary. The intention is more painterly, I think, than educational, and the book is constructed of quickly sketched scenes that serve both as a relief from the somber mood of the first and third books and also as a representation of that ideal of country life that was one of the fundamental promptings of the poem. The book closes with a paean to the almost idyllic existence of farmers who have "mastered their fears and fate's intransigence" and are friends of Pan, Sylvanus, and the sisterhood of nymphs. We may read the instructions for pruning grape vines with the distracted attention of a city dweller turning the pages and flipping through gardening catalogues—and if we do not necessarily feel any commitment to get out there and do any of those things, we are nonetheless happy merely to imagine, in an alternative life, some better version of ourselves that could do more than browse.

There is some such mechanism at work, clearly, for we indulge Virgil, allowing him to ramble on about such dreary subjects as the way to tell whether soil is too sandy or too loamy. He is, we understand, showing off more than a little, flaunting information he's picked up in his researches, the homelier the better. He takes care, for example, to mention that it is a good thing to spread manure on one's fields (2.346), but this earthiness is mostly a pose and never quite convincing. That unconvincingness becomes, after a time, the vehicle of a covert message—that the description of agricultural labor is turned into a piece of literary labor and, in a sense, its equivalent. Even if we should perhaps prefer to ignore the tawdry, Grub Street aspects of the literary life, Virgil calls our attention to them with his addresses to Maecenas, which occur in every book, and to Augustus Caesar in the first and third. There is a Lucretian precedent for these invocations, but Virgil's repetition of these ceremonial gestures also serves to bring his predicament into the poem. He is trying to make a living, serving one grand patron and hoping for another and even grander.

This pitch for commissions, or at least this admission that the poet is working for hire, trying to coax from unpromising and intractable material something tolerably diverting (to himself, first of all, but to us as well) is what gives some of his little embellishments and rhetorical flights their curious charm. He has, for example, a passage of jingoist boasting about Italy's superiority to all other countries:

> But neither the most fertile groves of the Medes
> Nor the beautiful Ganges, nor Hermus, turbid with gold,
> Can contend in praises with Italy, not Bactria, no,
> Nor the Indies, nor all of Panchaia so rich in incense. . . .
>
> [2.136–39]

It would be tempting to point to such passages, and there are a fair number of them, and use them to try to justify the poem. Any work that has so many excerptable sections, so many pieces calling out to be included in anthologies, has to be good, doesn't it? Well, that's true enough. But such a strategy is unnecessarily defensive and misses the structural virtues of the poem as a whole, which has a dramatic integrity that ought not be ignored. The poem is about the place of man in the universe, and its appeal is to the accomplishments and consolations of labor—which it not only recommends but exemplifies. The performance of the poet in a long, demanding, almost insane task, the writing of a poem to praise farming and instruct in its mysteries, is what we keep noticing and admiring, for along with these other rhetorical gestures, there is the artifactual sheen of the versification that calls attention to itself. We notice this elegance and have to ask ourselves what its purpose might possibly be. What farmer is going to care about this adventitious excellence? How is it useful or relevant? The answer, which lies at the heart of the poem's mystery, is that there is a craftsman's pride in the workmanship which is, in and of itself, a solace and a reward.

It is also difficult to talk about. There is, more often than critics would like to admit, a basic distortion in the explication and critical discussion of a literary work of art because, while the language may seem to be the same as in a poem, the in-

tentions and expectations of the poet and the writer are altogether different. The critic's job is explanation, the clarification
of what had been complicated or clouded before, or the resolution of perplexities and ambiguities. On the other side, one
of the possible ideals of the working artist is a clarity that does
not require any further comment and before which there is
almost nothing to say.

The poetry of Robert Herrick has probably been slighted
by academics and has been written about and taught less often
than one might have expected for work of such quality, not
out of spite or as a result of any conspiracy, but only because
a teacher would find it awkward and embarrassing to hold a
series of classes on these delicate and splendid poems. They
aren't difficult to understand. Their quality is impressive and
the pieces are often irresistible. But one can't simply exclaim
in admiration that, yes, this is fine, and then this next one is
also fine, and the next is just splendid. . . . It is possible to
make some technical remarks, of course, about some of the
prosodic and rhetorical strategies, but these explain too little
or too much and miss the point. Such trade secrets don't, in
the end, explain or even reveal, any more than a look at the
brand names and the shades of the cosmetics on a woman's
vanity table can explain her beauty.

Virgil, an extremely complex and self-conscious artist,
isn't much like Herrick, and in Virgil's work there is, most of
the time, a lot to talk about. But it is a mark of his achievement
in book 2 of the *Georgics* that the suave surface of the verse
doesn't invite or even permit much in the way of critical performance. It is only at the end, in the famous passage in praise
of country life, that we get something to chew on. There, the
tripartite construction may be clear, for there are the compar-
isons of city luxuries with country sufficiencies; of intellection
with faith and the knowledge of the gods; and of urbane ambition with innocent rural satisfactions. There is a precedent
in Hesiod's description (*Works and Days* 582–96) of the farmers'
respite during the dog days, which is in contrast to the ar-

duousness of the rest of what his poem describes. And it has been suggested that this passage works in the same way in Virgil's poem, offering a comparable moment of ideal repose, a counterpoise to the downwardness of the rest of the work.

> How fine it is to gaze at the waving box trees
> Of Cytorus, or stroll in the south, in Narycia, among
> The fragrant pines where the spongy ground owes
> nothing
> To the labors of men and the clank of their scrabbling
> tools.
>
> [2.437–39]

One can set essay questions, asking students to compare and contrast this passage with the section in book 1 that recounts the fall from the original state of Saturnian grace to the present arrangement, and there would be a long tradition of such exercises. Quintilian himself proposed as a subject for rhetorical exercises the comparison between city and country life, which is what Virgil is showing us here. There may even have been something of a joking overtone to the passage, a conspiratorial wink between the poet and certain knowing members of his audience who recognize that—oh no!—he's not giving us that old stuff again, is he?

What saves the passage, aside from the fact that it is so proficiently performed, is its placement and function in the architecture of the poem. The genial air of the book has led us, if we have been paying proper attention, to expect some such epitomization and, yes, here it comes. The fashions and caprices of urban life give way before the longer views of the countryside, and the landscapes, even if they are rather idealized, seem to hold out a promise of what a life can be, or perhaps an indictment of our so much more nervous and speculative careers.

> If there's no big house with imposing portals, and no
> Enormous tide of chattering guests disgorged

Every morning to lean on the inlaid pillars,
He doesn't care. The homespun he's pleased to wear
May not be tinted with pricey imported snake-spit,
As the oil in his larder isn't perfumed with spice—
Whichever one is the rage this season. He's dumb?
Perhaps, but he won't be made a fool of either—
A fair exchange.

[2.460–67]

The subtext of course is that while the country may be poor
and may demand arduous labor, the demands of the city are
even worse, less onerous physically perhaps but more cor-
rosive of the spirit. Virgil's work, in a general way, is mournful, so that even its exuberant moments acknowledge their
eccentricity and rarity.

It is interesting to compare Virgil's descriptions of farming with those of a poet who actually knows what he is talking
about—with the work, for instance, of Stephen Duck who, in
the early eighteenth century, was called, with some conde-
scension, the "thresher poet" because he actually worked as
a farmhand. The title page of his first collection of poems announced that he was

for many Years a poor Thresher in a Barn, at Charleton
in the County of Wilts, at the Wages of four Shillings and
Sixpence per Week, 'till taken Notice of by Her late Majesty Queen Caroline; who on Account of his great Genius, gave him an Apartment at Kew, near Richmond, in
Surry, and a Salary of Thirty Pounds per Annum; after
which he studied the learned Languages, took Orders,
and is now a dignified Clergyman.

When Duck wrote about agricultural work, he did so out of
direct experience, and there was, at least at the beginning of
his career, an unimpeachable authority to his poetry. "The
Thresher's Labour" was written while he was still a thresher:

Let those who feast at Ease on dainty Fare
Pity the Reapers, who their Feasts prepare:
For Toils scarce ever ceasing press us now;
Rest never does, but on the Sabbath, show:
And barely that our Masters will allow.
Think what a painful Life we daily lead;
Each morning early rise, go late to Bed;
Nor, when asleep, are we secure from Pain;
We then perform our Labours o'er again:
Our mimic Fancy ever restless seems;
And what we act awake, she acts in Dreams . . .
Thus, as the Year's revolving course goes round,
No respite from our Labour can be found;
Like Sisyphus, our Work is never done;
Continually rolls back the restless Stone.
New growing Labours still succeed the past;
And growing always new, must always last.

Raymond Williams, in his discussion of Duck's career in
The Country and the City, compares this early work with what
came later, after the poet had been taken up by the amused
nobility. Here is a sample of *Gratitude, a Pastoral*:

O You, MENALCAS, know my abject Birth,
Born in a Cot, and bred to till the Earth:
On rigid Worldlings always doom'd to wait,
Forc'd at their frugal Hands my bread to get:
But when my Wants to CAROLINE were known,
she bless'd me with a Pasture of my own.
This makes new Pleasures in my Bosom glow;
These joyful Looks I to her Bounty owe.

And, a year or two later, he is writing this way, in a piece
called "On Richmond Park and Royal Gardens":

Of blissful Groves I sing, and flow'ry Plains:
Ye Sylvan Nymphs, assist my rural strains.

What has happened is that Duck's own experience has given way to the Virgilian idealization of that experience. In just this way, A. J. Liebling found that soldiers in World War II who were coming under fire for the first time were likelier than not to assert that the experience was "just like in the movies," in yet another demonstration that life imitates art.

What Virgil did was virtually to invent the countryside, and that he did so out of whole cloth—or papyrus—is especially impressive when we see the dominance of his construction over the actual encounter of a working thresher with the tasks of agriculture. Even more important than the thinking is the framework for thought, and it is this framework that Virgil gave to Western civilization. His descriptions in *Georgic* 2 became prescriptions, and their cheerful quality is appropriate, coming as it does from their conquest of brute fact. Wherever Virgil was getting these details, he was watching the pages accumulate as the verse stretched out line after elegant line, more and more persuasive as it acquired bulk.

There are, in the confrontation of any writer with a blank page, the dire and disabling questions: what do I know about this, and how can I presume to speak with authority on such a subject? Knowledge is never a sufficient armament for these encounters. What is required, finally, is courage—or maybe mere brashness—and will. Virgil must have had such doubts, venturing as he was upon the most unpromising and uncongenial territory and bringing his bookishness to bear on the most recalcitrant material. There is a feeling of achievement we get in book 2, which is right, for it was perhaps the most difficult book to do. The first book came first, and Virgil was fresh and undaunted. Books 3 and 4 have a fair amount of narrative in them, from which there is a kind of architectural support. Or at least a little momentum. But in book 2, there is only one dumb piece of information about farming and then another one, and from this Virgil found himself making one plausible thirty-line passage and then another, and then another.

It hangs together by paragraphs, each of which is a small set piece. But the paragraphs fit together and enliven one another, like the splotches of paint on an abstract canvas. The readers' guides and Cliffs notes that outline the argument of the poem miss the point entirely, because the argument is only there as a pretext. The real text is in the juxtaposition of timbres and textures and colorations, the emotional and affective implications of this piece and then that, and—preeminently—of the modulation from the first piece to the second.

Let us consider a characteristic passage, a discussion of the depth to which one ought to plant vines and trees. The advice is, on its face, useless, because no one who was about to undertake such a project as putting a grape vine or a tree into the earth would need to know that the trench for the vine ought to be "shallow" while the hole for the tree should be "deeper." The imparting of information, however, is not the point. What Virgil tells us is:

Maybe you'll ask how deep to make your trenches.
I'd suggest you set your vines in a shallow
Furrow. A tree would be planted deeper, low
In the earth, especially oak, that raises its crown
As high in the airy skies as it sinks its roots
Downward to Tartarus. Neither winter's storms
Nor showers can overturn it, but it persists,
Unmoved for years as the ages of men progress,
But it endures, waiting us out and winning,
Extending its arms and branches this way and that
And offering us its parasol of shade.

[2.288–97]

Well, there you are, with your shovel, ready to dig a hole to put your vine cutting into the earth, and all you get is a disquisition on how the hole ought to be shallower than what you'd make if you were going to put in an oak tree. But not quite all, for then there is the riff, the little cadenza on the oak tree's contrariness, with its crown going as high as its roots go deep. It lives a long time and outlasts men, so that it wins (*vincit*), which seems adversarial or even hostile. But then it turns out to be benign, because it offers us shade with its strong, protective branches.

These are not huge and dramatic gestures, but they fit into the rhythm of the poem and its alternation of dominant and tonic emotional chords. The high/low contrariety which turns into that of good/bad which is the guts of the passage is not intended as any serious moral examination of an oak tree, either, but is a rhetorical exercise. Finally, we are invited to look beyond holes in the dirt and beyond oak trees to the figure at the library table, turning out his tropes and spinning out his lines. The trick in which the magician produces the endless stream of colored handkerchiefs from the empty cannister isn't about fabric or handkerchiefs or cannisters, or even in the long run about prestidigitation, but about him, his authority, his formal clothes, his suave demeanor, his defiance, however momentary and illusory, of the limitations of the human condition.

THE HUSBANDRY OF GRIEF

The third book of the *Georgics* has an elaborate proem perhaps influenced by the odes of Pindar, or at least the Pindaric conceit of the chariot of song. Virgil begins by invoking the gods of herds and flocks, but then, changing direction, he announces that he will make a monument to Caesar and his victories in battle. This may or may not have been intended as a piece of self-promotion, a prospectus for what eventually became the *Aeneid*. It is almost impossible, however, to look back from our vantage point without interpreting this passage as a kind of announcement of Virgil's poetic ambition and, more pointedly, as a solicitation of patronage and support. These are subjects that would be intrusive if the poem were actually about farming, but that pretense is less and less necessary to maintain. The poem has established itself and, from this point forward, Virgil lets it run, taking him and us wherever it seems willing to go. The accomplishment is secure enough so that, as with the *Eclogues*, there is no need for any slavish observance of the conventions.

The discussion of horses and cattle which occupies the next couple of hundred lines is only partially relevant to agriculture. Horses were hardly farm animals in Italy. They were used for military service, for racing, and for some hauling— although on farms, most of the hauling was done by oxen. If Virgil were addressing plausible farmers, we might expect some talk of pigs, perhaps, but the possible gain in verisimilitude of such a passage would not have been offset by the loss of *dignitas* or the violation of decorum. Horses are more heroic and, well, honorable. Far better to talk about them. They're still animals—and smart readers can generalize, can't they?

Because they are animals, they allow Virgil to address himself to two of the irrational wildernesses that limit the world of work and its rationality—the unyielding imponderabilities of lust and death that can obtrude at any time upon any of us. These subjects interest him, as the actual work of the livestock breeders does not. Or, to put it another way, there is more of a connection now between his real and ostensible subject, between text and pretext, than there was in the *Eclogues*, where, let us remember, Virgil was describing shepherds and goatherds, people who were presumably engaged in the same occupation as the one upon which he now discourses. He took little notice, in the earlier work, of what these herdsmen actually did. He takes more now—but only a little. One needn't be a sophisticated student of modern genetics to see that his approach is, to say the least, selective. He suggests that in selecting cattle for breeding purposes, one must look to the dams (3.51); for breeding horses, one looks to the sires (3.72ff.).

Horses and cows have almost nothing to do with what is on Virgil's mind, however. He is talking about the griefs of

the flesh, the upsurge of health and strength in an animal's
youth, and then the long and inexorable decline. It is in the
course of this exposition that we get the lines that Dr. Johnson
thought were so moving:

> optima quaeque dies miseris mortalibus aevi
> prima fugit: subeunt morbi tristisque senectus
> et labor, et durae rapit inclementia mortis.

> (For wretched mortals the best days are the first
> And soon disappear; then come sickness and gloomy
> Age, and pains, until implacable death
> Takes us away.)

[3.66–68]

It has been remarked that, in this book, Virgil uses a
somewhat broader brush than in the first two. The sections
are larger, depending less on the accumulation of discrete details than on the larger logical and emotional units that are the
building blocks of the poem. He can afford to relax a bit now,
for the difficult books are behind him. Sex and death are meat
and drink to poets (what else is so interesting, after all?). And
there was, we may suppose, an outline for book 4 with its
stretch of narrative, the myth that was to end the poem in
much the same way that the myth ends Plato's *Republic,* moving the discourse to a new and, in some senses, higher plane.

It is also a safe inference to draw, considering the rest of
Virgil's work, that he found the minor key of this book comfortable, its complaints being well within the tessitura of his
poetic voice. His warning about the physical toll of sexual activity seems to extend beyond the merely physical and well
beyond the subject at hand, which is, after all, animal husbandry.

> There is no better way to improve an animal's strength
> Than abstinence, to avoid the goads of lust,
> Whether it's bulls or stallions you're trying to breed.
> That's why they send the bull to some lonely pasture

All the way off, on the other side of the mountain,
Or across the river, or keep him shut up in the stall,
For the female saps his strength inexorably
As he stares at her. He's consumed with longing, melts
Like a burning candle, forgets the meadows and
    groves. . . .

                                        [3.209–16]

The celebration of the power of sex is never stronger than in these prohibitions—one thinks of the behavior of certain conservative religious groups, whether Christian, Moslem, or Jewish, that separate the sexes, that require women to cover their hair or their faces, or their upper arms, and one realizes that those are the people who recognized the force of sexuality. Ovid plays with sexuality and tries to turn it into a joke, which is a way of diminishing something that, otherwise, might be frightening. Virgil is not at all playful, and the respect he pays to sex is therefore all the more powerful and impressive. This is the tone, after all, of *Eclogue* 10—which recounted and mourned the fate of Gallus, Virgil's friend, who came to grief through an unfortunate liaison.

The parallels are more than casual. Ruined by his disastrous love for Cytheris, Gallus went off to find the solace of physical hardship in hunting and military service in the sleet and blizzards of Macedonia, or to herd sheep under the sweltering African sun (*Eclogue* 10.65–69). In the same way, the bulls fight for the desirable heifer, gore each other in their furious battle, and then:

The loser goes off to lick his wounds in distant
And unknown regions, groaning in pain and chagrin
The victor inflicted upon him. He goes into training,
Swaps his comfy stall for a makeshift bed
On flint and feeds on the rough reed-grasses.
With his horns, he butts and gores saplings and trees
In practice, to vent his rage. He paws the ground

And tosses the sand in anger, collecting his strength
For the rematch that is to come.

[3.225–35]

This is not an isolated horror, either, but a general rule, as
Virgil makes clear—"amor omnibus idem," love is the same
for all (3.244). When we think of Virgil's most famous love
story, that of Dido and Aeneas, we must realize that, among
other things, the poet probably meant to demonstrate his hero's strength of character in not giving in to the promptings
of his emotions.

Indeed, the pretense at describing the care, feeding, and
breeding of animals is abandoned entirely by line 257, when
we get the story of Hero and Leander, not named except as
"the youth" and "the maiden," but we know the story, which
is to say we know its moral perfectly well, too. Virgil refers to
that story, then refers to the story of Glaucus, the son of Sisyphus, king of Corinth, by Merope, the daughter of Atlas,
whose mares tore him apart because Venus had driven them
crazy. Why? Virgil doesn't go into details, but rather he assumes that we know them. We are supposed to reflect on how
Glaucus kept his mares away from his stallions so as to make
the horses of both gender run faster. And the enraged mares
ripped him limb from limb.

The climax, as it were, of this section on lust, now that
the poem has returned to the subject of mares, is the report
of how, in estrus, they can turn their hindquarters into the
breeze and get themselves impregnated by the wind, alone.
It is a mystery, a dark mystery, magic, and there are spells
that some wicked old women know how to cast using the
menstrual blood of horses and turning its power to affect the
lives of men. But having alluded in that way, en passant, to
such a subject, Virgil goes on to the second part of the book,
about sheep and goats, how their pens should have plenty of
bracken, and how to prevent foot-rot.

This is, of course, an interlude, a brief respite from the

heaviness that we have just negotiated and the even heavier subject that the poem has in store for us. What we are working up to is the account of the plague, modeled on that of Lucretius at the end of book 6 of *De rerum natura* (which, in turn, was probably modeled on Thucydides' account of the plague at Athens of 430 B.C.). Lucretius gives a dismaying abundance of vivid details of a plague that is all the more effective for its laconic objectivity. In an almost reportorial tone, he sets forth the evidence he allows his readers to interpret. The emotional valence of these details is assumed. Such restraint would have been rather confining for Virgil, but he begins nevertheless in a markedly Lucretian manner, expository and didactic if not actually professorial: "Diseases also will I explain, their causes, signs and symptoms" (3.440). It sounds more than accidentally reminiscent of the line in Lucretius in which the earlier poet introduces his concluding section: "I will now explain the nature of epidemics and the source from which the cumulative power of pestilence can bring a sudden and ruinous plague on the tribes of men and beasts" (6.1090–93). In this guise of instructor, Virgil can give advice and warn what the consequences may be of ignoring his precautions, but that is hardly the point. For one thing, there aren't any precautions that work. There isn't any safety and, all too often, there is nothing to be done.

The aesthetic point is clear, however. There are 125 lines of one degree or another of horrors, which is nearly a quarter of book 3. This is a large structural element and it serves at least two functions, first bringing the discussion of animal husbandry to a full stop on as somber a note as can be imagined, and then providing the basis for the reorganization and leap into faith of book 4.

Robert Penn Warren used to tell his students that a short story was, essentially, a moment of re-vision, a shift from the first glimpse of some character or situation to another and, presumably, deeper or more important truth. It is an interesting theory and it accommodates some stories better than

others, but it seems relevant here to Virgil's program in the
Georgics. The first truth to be asserted is the gloomy view of
sex and death in book 3. They are, indeed, risky and ruinous,
and Virgil is eloquently mournful as he describes the deaths
not only of single animals but of whole herds:

> Cures they invented killed, and the healers gave up,
> Chiron, Phillyra's son, and Melampus, Amythaon's.
> Wan Tisiphone came from the black depths
> Of the underworld, with Fear and Plague outriding,
> Raising her head higher daily and hungrier.
> Bleatings and mournful mooings arise, a sad
> Chorus, from streams, from riverbanks, and from hills
> On which whole herds died, and their corpses rotted
> And stank to high heaven even in the sheep folds.
> They had to be buried in pits.

> [3.549–58]

It is a dismal business, and Virgil piles detail upon detail,
but where he ends up is back in the world of men:

> Even the fleeces were useless. No one could wear them:
> They were so corrupted with pus that the wool would rot
> On the warp of the loom. But if you could manage
>   to weave
> Some kind of garment and wear it, you'd break out
>   in boils;
> Then fevers and sweats would seize you; your limbs
>   would burn,
> And the curse, in very short order, consumed your flesh.

> [3.559–65]

The informed guess about this disease is that it is not bu-
bonic plague but, more likely, erysipelas, a strep infection that
is highly contagious and, in such forms as gangrenous erysipelas, is still described as "always fatal." There is a genus of
microorganisms of the family Corynebacteriaceae, order Eu-

bacteriales, which contains a single species, *Erysiplothrix in-sidiosa*, a species occurring as Gram-positive rods and filaments that is the causative agent of swine erysipelas "and also infecting sheep, turkeys, and rats" (*Dorland's Illustrated Medical Dictionary*, 24th edition). This form of the disease is contagious to man from contact with "infected meat, hides, or bones"—pretty much as Virgil reports.

But having said that, I am forced to stop and ask myself what difference it makes that Virgil and his sources happened to be accurate with this particular piece of information. If there were no such disease, would the emotional impact of the passage be any the less? Or if we had no idea which disease it might have been that he was talking about? In the next book, on apiculture, Virgil does a number about the war of the king bees that is purely and grandly wrong. The idea that the huge fat bee might be a female and that the other bees might be the workers and the male drones was . . . impossible. So Virgil wrote about the battle of the king bees, for which lapse we somewhat condescendingly forgive him.

On the other hand, when he gets his information right, or we can contrive to explain away the discrepancies, the temptation is to take these instances of accuracy or luck as indicators of worth. We shouldn't. We can quite easily imagine a much more accurate but less valuable literary work. The appeal to external truth, to the truth of correspondence, is a fundamentally vulgar exercise, after all, the kind of thing certain popular novelists rely on to fascinate those readers for whom the more literary truths of coherence are inaccessible or ineffective.

The point was and still is the making of a poem with its rhetorical and metrical structures working their affective magic. That the material has been scrounged from the available sources is a part of the magic—the bringing to life of these pieces of dead texts being exactly the kind of triumph Dr. Frankenstein was trying for.

The declaration Virgil made in book 2 was clear enough:

First, before anything else, let the sweet Muses
Welcome me, whose secrets I worship, stricken,
Their adoring acolyte, and let poetry show me
The ways of the stars in heaven, the sun's eclipses,
And the moon's courses.

[2.475–78]

The poetry, in other words, is primary, and the natural science is the secondary consideration.

So long as we keep this priority clear in our minds, we are unlikely to misread the *Georgics*. The poem is a representation of Virgil's understanding of life itself, a mixture of small victories and large disasters, and the emotional and structural requirements of this representation are what determine that there should be a description of dying animals at the end of the third book. The real purpose is to echo and intensify the descriptions of natural and supernatural portents of disaster at the end of book 1. This picture of contagion, suffering, and death is the low point of the poem, which is the prerequisite for the ascent of book 4. It is grim, stark, and its pretense is a lack of artifice, particularly in the way the book ends, just breaking off as if the poet didn't have the heart to go on.

THE MIRACLE OF CREATION

It was Lazzaro Spallanzani, the eighteenth-century Italian physiologist, who devised the experiments finally to disprove the notion of spontaneous generation. Those maggots didn't just arise from the rotting meat but were, as he demonstrated, the natural result of eggs laid by flying insects. Whether Virgil would have been surprised by these findings is a difficult question, but the belief in that kind of generation of insects, and of bees in particular, was certainly widespread. We now know better, but our sophistication is useful only if we understand that the fourth book of the *Georgics* is already nudging

at the limits of nature. Virgil's linking of the Aristaeus story
with that of Orpheus and Eurydice makes it clear that he is
deliberately venturing beyond the borders of ordinary experience and into the realm of the supernatural. Or, putting it
another way, he is exploring the confines of reason and step-
ping, or leaping, beyond and into the territory of faith.

The fourth book of the *Georgics*, Servius reports, is a re-
write of what was, in an earlier version, praise of Virgil's old
friend Gallus. If we can believe this account, the part about
Gallus took up the entire second half of the book, but then
came Gallus's disgrace, suicide, and *damnatio memoriae* (an
expunging of all reference to the name of the deceased—a
technique the Soviets revived in our time). Virgil prudently
substituted the story of Aristaeus, putting in the business
about the regeneration of the bees. He had no particular desire
to join his old pal among the ranks of nonpersons. Whatever
resurrections Virgil was going to attempt, they would be general and abstract.

It is a difficult thing to imagine what the fourth book
would have been in its first version, or how Maecenas and
Augustus would have reacted to so bizarre a concluding gesture—however much Virgil liked the man or admired him as
a poet or statesman, Gallus was far less important than Maecenas or the emperor. And the *Georgics* was no private piece
of musing, but a very public poem.

It has been suggested, however implausibly, that Servius
perhaps got the *Eclogues* and the *Georgics* confused. Or that
there might even have been some reference of a few lines to
Gallus that might have occurred at the introduction of the
Aristaeus section, which would have been à propos because
Virgil attributes the mysterious practice of "bougonia," or bee-
generation, to Egypt, where Gallus was governor general.
And it is quite conceivable that such a reference was there and
was excised in a politic redaction.

I much prefer this view, mostly because I like the poem
the way it is and find it impossible to imagine any other set of

gestures that would conclude the work in so satisfying a manner. The main trick of writing is to learn to read well, to see what possibilities arise from the gestures one has already made, to respond properly to these suggestions, and therefore to improve upon anything one might have excogitated ex nihilo. The outline is there to be improved upon, not altogether forgotten or discarded but not binding either, so that what one learns from the text ought to be put to use for the benefit of both the artist and the work of art. The first 1,500 lines of a poem ought to give us a fair idea of the range and direction of the concluding 566. Taking music as the model, we ought to have a certain set of expectations if only to have them at the same time satisfied and exceeded. The conclusion of the *Georgics* is satisfying in that way, and our expectations are surely exceeded as Virgil shifts into his mythopoeic mode.

The choice of beekeeping as a subject was surely a calculated one, for it allowed a number of elegant moves—bees with their special relation to Jupiter have been granted particular privileges in the animal world, and theirs is an ordered society, a model of divine logos. Their honey is practical and useful, and indeed was the only sweetener the Romans had for their cooking. Beyond its utility, however, there was an obvious metaphorical suggestiveness. And, finally, the notion about how bees could be generated from rotting corpses gave Virgil exactly the right mixture of the practical and the exotic, with an opportunity for him to blossom from the didactic and expository into the narrative voice.

Some of this—we have no way of guessing—comes from a lost poem of Nicander's about bees and beekeeping that, according to Quintilian, Virgil used as his source for this book, as he is said to have used material from Aratus in the first book. But what that poem was like is impossible to say. It is convenient, however, to have some lost precedent, some authority for Virgil's mistakes—the war of the king bees, for instance, that comes up fairly early on, seems now to be rather an awkward error. King bees? But the notion of scientific accuracy and experimental verification as being superior to the following of authority and precedent is a relatively recent intellectual fetish. To medieval writers, the notion of consulting nature directly was just a bit vulgar. What was the point of having learned how to read if you could go out and stand in a field to find this stuff out? Where was the satisfaction of finding just the right reference in an all but forgotten book to confound one's adversaries and establish the superiority of one's own learning? All you need to be a scientist is to be an acute observer; to be a scholar, you have to know how to read texts and you have to remember them!

So, let us suppose it was Nicander who had interesting things to say about the war of the king bees and even about the rotting-beef method of generation of insect life, and let us imagine that Virgil was reading along in his copy of Nicander's work for the details that he wanted in order to complete his poem. Does that make it better or worse? If we were to imagine a work of Nicander's that was accurate in every detail, so that all the errors were Virgil's, would that be relevant? The point, I think, is that it doesn't matter. The material is sufficiently unpromising and absurd, and the transformation is grand enough for us to admire the poem, whether we choose to do so in spite of its inaccuracies or because of them. The message of the poem, its largest motion and tendency, is the assertion of the possibility of the achievement of some kind of immortality through a work of labor and skill which we may prefer to call "art." And the brute fact is that Virgil has been dead for a couple of thousand years, and yet not dead. With its king bees for queens, the poem is healthy and thriving, in print and available both in its original Latin and in translations. Boys and girls and men and women who have never set foot on a farm and who are distressed to think that vegetables actually grow in the dirt somewhere have been reading these lines, the survival of which is a bizarre and all but unimaginable fulfillment of the poet's vatic pronouncement that death is, in some sense, conquerable. That this triumph has been achieved with such materials, absurdly unpromising at the time and, as we now know, even erroneous and therefore all the more absurd, returns our attention—or ought to—to the achievement of the poesis itself.

Individual bees die but the hive continues and enjoys, in a sense, a kind of immortality. Their buzz continues and survives unchanged. Our cultural emphasis on the individual and individual salvation, and our corresponding deemphasis of—and even failure of belief in—the salvation of the whole group, is a relatively recent development. The terrors of excommunication were grounded precisely upon that all but lost idea of the community as the appropriate and likely vehicle of salvation and redemption. It is such an idea of community that Virgil is surely invoking here, that sense of the communal life to which a serious contemplation of the organized society of the beehive inevitably gives rise.

This kind of metaphoric suggestion and its wonderful opportunity for conversion of the humble if not actually dreary details of farmers' lore into social and philosophical comment must have been delightful for Virgil to contemplate, and there is a playful grandiloquence to his descriptions of the social organization of the beehive that invites us to share his delight:

A trivial subject, you'd think, but glory is never
A trivial thing, if only I do it right
And Apollo hears my plea and comes to my aid.
                                                          [4.6–7]

Apollo seems generously disposed. And Virgil is obviously having a very good time for himself. There is, for one thing, the sense of accomplishment and the imminent completion of the poem. Virgil compares himself to a a sailor furling his sails and turning his prow to land. But mostly one has the sense that he is comfortable with the material, that he likes the effortlessness of the poetic maneuvering. He doesn't have to push much for significance beyond the strictly apicultural:

> Neither in Egypt nor mighty Lydia, nor Parthia, nor
> Among the Medes is there paid such reverence to kings
> As what the bees display. If their king is safe,
> All is well, but if he's lost, they're lost.
> He is the lord of all their works, and to him
> They look and crowd about him, lifting him up
> On their shoulders or, serving as shields, they keep
>   him safe,
> Risking their own bodies, eager for wounds
> Or even a glorious death for the sake of their king.
>
> [4.209–18]

Day-Lewis found this passage so embarrassing that he quietly corrected "king" to "queen," which was important only if one assumed that the poem was actually about bees.

For the first 280 lines Virgil maintains that possibility, but then he moves to his coda, turning to the myth, cutting to the chase—and clothing his meaning in such regalia as to allow us considerable leeway in our interpretation of how, precisely, we are to understand the Aristaeus story, or the Orpheus story, or the relevance of both of them to the work as a whole. It is helpful to know that the formal and structural requirements of the epyllion seemed to be such as to demand exactly that kind of story-within-a-story as we get here. The contrasting inset, as L. P. Wilkinson points out, is a feature not only of Callimachus's *Hecale*, which is probably the prototype, but also of Moschus's *Europa* and of Catullus's *Peleus and Thetis*. In the Moschus piece, there is a description of the heroine's basket that has on it a depiction of the story of Io being turned into a heifer and driven away by Hera, and in the Catullus work there is the marriage coverlet with a depiction of the story of Ariadne that covers more than half of the poem.

These internal set pieces are related to the main stories, but the connection can be thematic and the effect can be one of contrast. The connection in the *Georgics* seems clear enough —the restoration of life, whether that of the bees or of Or-

pheus's beloved Eurydice, and the triumph of art. Indeed, the
restoration of life *is* the triumph of art, or at least is the measure by which the art is finally to be judged. It is not certain
whether Virgil was following some lost tradition or was add-
ing his own embellishment in having Orpheus look back at
Eurydice and lose her. In the normal version of the story, Orpheus was successful. (Only in Plato's *Symposium* do we get
a variation in which Orpheus gets to see only a wraith of his
wife because he is not brave enough to go down to Hades.)
But the ambiguous victory Virgil contrives is better than
none—and more plausible than any complete and unambig-
uous success would have been. Poets don't just conjure up
dead people, after all, and to claim that they do or even that
the proto-poet could have done so by his singing, would simply not be credible. But to suggest that such a thing can happen—or at the least can seem to happen—for a wonderful and
heartbreakingly brief moment is to affirm a truth all of us can
recognize and yield to.

The subject of the powers of art and the limits of those
powers was central to the *Eclogues* and it has not been abandoned here but, rather, is addressed in a new and more
profound way. The triumph of art, which is order and artic-
ulation, over death's mess is central to the Orpheus story, of
course, but it is also the practical basis for the Aristaeus story.
The shamanic descent of Aristaeus into the waters, which is
suggestive of Orpheus's descent, may have been adapted
from the story of Theseus's visit to his stepmother, Amphi-
trite. Aristaeus too was the son of a nymph, Cyrene. His descent into the sea and the trials of his encounter with Proteus
amount to a kind of initiation ordeal that may well have had
some connection with the practices of one or another of the
mystery cults such as that of Eleusis.

What Proteus reveals is that Orpheus sent the punishment and must now be propitiated—which seems, otherwise,
irrelevant, because Cyrene seems to have known all along
how to recreate the life of the bees. There is a mechanical con-

nection that the narrative offers in the information about Eurydice having met her death by snakebite because she was fleeing from Aristaeus, but this is a mere detail and hardly compelling. What works, persuading us so that we don't question too closely these narrative links, is the general sense of the mysterious descent and ordeal. Whether or not this process is related in some way to the mystery cults, there is a more general psychic truth that has been announced by any number of poets, Rilke perhaps as eloquent as any, to the effect that what poetry demands is that you change your life.

There is a dark night of the soul through which some writers go, and it does change them. And they are, afterwards, able to see what was at hand all along but could not speak to them—as, for instance, the instructions of Cyrene about what to do to prepare the sacrifice. The story Proteus tells is that of the miracle of Orpheus's re-creation of Eurydice, which would have been successful—or actually was successful, except for his failure of faith in what he was doing. He turned and looked back, and that lapse was fatal:

> In that one moment was all his labor lost
> And his covenant with the stern king violated.
> Three times the fatal thunder crashed and the dark
> Pool of Avernus echoed.
>
> [4.490–92]

Awesome. Wonderful and terrible. For the first loss was now compounded and for this new bereavement Orpheus held himself responsible.

Small wonder that his grief this time was unassuaged and that he could do nothing but lament. "Neither love nor marriage could sway his soul," Virgil has Proteus report. And in the madness of his grief, Orpheus is not altogether different from Virgil's old friend Gallus, for Proteus tells us how the proto-poet "roamed the fields of northern ice, the cold / Banks of the Don, the frosty mountain passes." Outraged at such excess, the Thracian matrons rip Orpheus limb from limb, but his severed head continues to sing for his lost Eurydice.

This too is a curious state of affairs. The Thracian matrons would presumably have approved of Orpheus's love for a living Eurydice, but his total absorption in lamentation, which is, after all, another aspect of poesis, might have been offensive to them, unnatural at least in the sense of its artifice, and perhaps also objectionable on the grounds of its sterility. One need not push too hard to think of the Thracian matrons as priestesses of some terrifying fertility cult, and Virgil allows us to do this, describing the women as "outraged / And at their sacred rites, their midnight / Bacchanals, they tore the youth apart."

It is a bizarre and disturbing story, but it must be accepted—which is, fundamentally, what is required of Aristaeus. One advantage of the epyllion with its story-within-a-story is that Virgil is enabled by the shape of the piece to contrive for Aristaeus a point of view which is more or less that of the reader. The reaction of Aristaeus is therefore, in some measure, ours as well, and the sacrifice he performs is on our behalf. The sacrifice, an act of reverence and adoration as well as of expiation, is a ritual acknowledgment of the holiness of Orpheus's exploit and his death. What is demanded is the outward show of an inner belief in the possibility of immortality through art—not its likelihood, necessarily, but its possibility. We must realize that poetry at least descends from magic and religion.

Proteus plunges back into the deep, and Cyrene tells her son what she may have known all along but was not, until this point, permitted to impart to him, instructing him in the necessary sacrifices he must make to the Dryads, and to the unreconciled shades of Orpheus and Eurydice. Then:

> Without delay, he executes these instructions
> His mother gave, goes to the shrines, erects
> The proper altars, leads out the four choice bulls,

Prime steers, and as many unyoked heifers.
Then, on the ninth dawn, when he returns
To the grove to offer Orpheus sacrifices,
He finds, *mirabile dictu*, the miraculous thing—
Bees buzzing, from inside the carcasses, swarming. . . .

[4.546–55]

It wasn't what Cyrene had promised. It isn't even clear that she knew what would happen. The miracle comes not from her but from some higher source, and is the reward for Aristaeus's piety, or at least, in some mysterious way, the acknowledgment of the earlier miracle enables the realization of this new one.

It has been pointed out that bees avoid carrion and that the entire event is not only unlikely but absurd. Scholars point out that in countries where there is a scarcity of trees, as for instance in Egypt, to which Virgil makes special reference, bees have been observed nesting in dried carcasses of animals. Samson, of course, finds a swarm of bees and honey in the carcass of a lion (Judges 14:8). But an alternative suggestion is that there is a remarkable resemblance between some bees and the drone fly, *Eristalis tenax*, which actually does lay its eggs in decomposing flesh of dead animals, on which its maggots then feed. Such speculations may be entertaining, but they have nothing to do with Virgil's poem.

Even if the prescription worked, it would be a fairly useless one—the sacrifice of the calf being disproportionately expensive. It would be cheaper simply to purchase new bees. The only value of the procedure is in the assertion that it is, contrary to all commonsense expectations, possible, that there is a mode of thought and therefore of existence in which mortality can be suspended, that there are some small precincts in which death shall have no dominion. The claim Virgil makes for poetry primarily, but by extension to all the crafts by which mankind distinguishes itself as *homo faber*, is that there is something that survives. Life may be brutish and

short, but there is, in cultivation—in all the different senses
of that word—something noble that extends beyond a lifetime
and can go on for generations, for thousands of years.

To that claim of longevity, even the most dour sceptic
must give assent, for he can see its proof before him, can look
at the text that has survived all this time and read for himself
the simple declaration of a mere matter of fact:

> Of agriculture, the care of flocks, the growing
> Of trees, I sang—while mighty Caesar brandished
> A sword at the far Euphrates, dispensing laws
> To grateful populations, in pleasant Naples
> All this time, I, Virgil, kept myself
> Busy obscurely with plowshares who used to dally
> With eclogues. O Tityrus, where are you now?
>
> [4.558–65]

PART III
THE AENEID

HAIL, CAESAR!

COMES, AT LAST, THE GREAT EPIC, THAT FAMOUS WORK, THE *Aeneid*, about which I think the first thing to be said is that it has an odd shape. It is as if, in *Ben Hur*, the chariot race came in the first twenty minutes. There is in the *Aeneid* an awesome intensity at the beginning: we get the wonderful first four books about the fall of Troy and Aeneas's flight, and then his dalliance with Dido and her suicide. Aeneas continues on with his travels and, in book 6, visits the underworld (this is another high point). Nothing in the second six books quite matches this, however, and while the campaign in Italy and the final struggle with Turnus may be interesting, there is nothing to quite satisfy the reader's expectation that the epic established with its dazzling opening.

What is required—what Virgil assumed and indeed demanded—is a reference on our part to something outside the poem. Epic is, after all, historical poetry, and Virgil was writing at a particular and remarkable moment in Roman history. Literature has its timeless aspect, but it also arises from particular lives and particular moments. Some of these are extraordinary, and it was Virgil's peculiar fate and fortune to have lived and written in one of those rare and most intense times when the darkness had, for a moment anyway, relented. After years of uncertainty, warfare, slaughter, and anarchy, Augustus Caesar had imposed upon the world a moment of order and peace. Instead of suffering and waste, there was stability and even a fair measure of justice.

We have had such a moment, recently. In that brief

glimpse of light when the Berlin Wall came down, when the iron curtain lifted, and when the strictures of apartheid began to relax in South Africa, our grim expectations of eventual ruin were at least for a few months suspended (until Iraq invaded Kuwait). That striking moment may have been ephemeral, but it was enough for us to entertain some dim notion of what it felt like to live at that moment in Augustan Rome. That principate was a time of so great and intense a hope that its memory has endured for millennia. The eighteenth-century British gentleman took the age of Augustus Caesar as his conscious model in literature and politics. Christianity itself is at least in part an expression of the hopefulness of that moment, the sense that there was a new dispensation in the world, a new possibility for the way men and women might conduct their affairs, an idea of the possibility of a relenting of savagery and a limit if not an end to barbarity and chaos.

That hopeful moment stands at the other end of the poem, and everything in the poem points toward it. To answer the grandeur of Troy and its towers, there is—not in the text but in the world around it—the grandeur of Augustus's government and his marble city on seven hills. One may indeed suggest that the strategy of the poem is to connect the present miracle with the earlier tradition of gods, demigods, heroes, and miracles. It was Virgil's bold suggestion that the mythic dimension was the necessary and proper way of understanding this remarkable development in the sorry story of mankind.

A lesser poet, a lesser thinker, would have produced a cheerier work, a kind of John Philip Sousa march in hexameters. What is extraordinary about the *Aeneid* is that, celebrating such a moment and such a ruler, it is so predominantly sad a poem. There is a tragic sense of the world's griefs, the costs of suffering and blood. After all, if the sky clears, there are two ways to think about the preceding darkness. One is, what a waste it was, how foolish and unnecessary. That's sad, but sadder yet is the alternative, that it was necessary, and how pitiable for those who suffered that they had to pay these terrible costs and had no idea that a better time was coming.

In the end, Aeneas is as pitiable as Turnus. Turnus dies, and at Aeneas's hand, but we feel sorry for both of them, understanding how their pride and implacable hatred have driven them to this sorry moment—in other words, how history and fate have borne upon them, forcing the hand that holds the gleaming blade. The *Aeneid* is a poem of the griefs that had gone before and would almost certainly come again— for Virgil's temperament was basically melancholy, and if he was too intelligent to minimize the blessings of the present moment, he was too shrewd to rely on their permanence. Augustus would die in his bed, but Tiberius, Domitian, Titus, Caligula, and Nero would supply the Romans with abundant demonstration that the end to cruelty and injustice had not yet arrived.

The *Aeneid* is a fundamentally conservative poem, celebrating what was and what is. It honors Augustus and his government, but there is also an implied demand upon him and his heirs—that they live up to the poem's expectations and justify the epic sufferings not only of Aeneas, but also of King Evander and his son Pallas, Amazon-like Camilla, desperate Mezentius, noble Turnus, poor Queen Amata, and the magnificent Dido. A realist, Virgil had to have known that the hopes the poem implies would be betrayed—but that one was nonetheless obliged to hope. This is, I think, the fundamental tension of the entire work, an agonized struggle between doubt and hope, as dirge and celebration shimmer and enliven the stately array of hexameter lines.

We take the *Aeneid* for granted, much as farmers who live beneath a promontory with some grand temple on its height come to take for granted the marvel tourists keep coming to see. It has become a fixture in our cultural landscape, which makes it harder rather than easier to see properly. What we must try to do—and are able to do at this odd moment in the crucial last decade of the twentieth century—is recreate the

hope and nervousness of Virgil's time and in our most alert
and anxious optimism allow the poem to resonate as it must
have resonated then.

The first book is action and adventure—a storm at sea,
catastrophe narrowly averted, landfall, and the introduction
of Dido. Then, in book 2, we get Aeneas's story that he recounts to Dido and the others gathered in her hall, the story
of the fall of Troy:

> "Sorrow too deep to tell, your majesty,
> You order me to feel and tell once more:
> How the Danaans leveled in the dust
> The splendor of our mourned-forever kingdom—
> Heartbreaking things I saw with my own eyes
> And was a part of. Who could tell them,
> Even a Myrmidon or Dolopian
> Or ruffian of Ulysses, without tears?
> Now, too, the night is well along, with dewfall
> Out of heaven, and setting stars weigh down
> Our heads toward sleep. But if so great desire
> Moves you to hear the tale of our disasters,
> Briefly recalled, the final throes of Troy,
> However I may shudder at the memory
> And shrink again in grief, let me begin."
>   [Fitzgerald, 2.3–17]

Virgil is establishing his authority and that of his narrator and
hero as well. The announcement that "I am going to tell you
something terrible" commands attention even now, but the
effect then was greater and clearer, for the established convention in tragedy was for a messenger to come running in to
tell the chorus and the audience whatever the dire news was
that lay at the heart of the drama. The main action was always
off stage (ob-scene) and was reported in words by the messenger, who usually made a few such prefatory remarks. In
Sophocles' *Antigone*, for instance, the messenger comes on to
say:

> Men of the line of Cadmos, you who live
> Near Amphion's citadel:
> > I cannot say
> Of any condition of human life "This is fixed,
> This is clearly good, or bad." Fate raises up,
> And Fate casts down the happy and unhappy alike:
> No man can foretell his Fate.
> > Take the case of Creon:
> Creon was happy once, as I count happiness:
> Victorious in battle, sole governor of the land,
> Fortunate father of children nobly born.
> And now it has all gone from him! Who can say
> That a man is still alive when his life's joy fails?
> He is a walking dead man. Grant him rich,
> Let him live like a king in his great house:
> If his pleasure is gone, I would not give
> So much as the shadow of smoke for all he owns.
> > [Fitts and Fitzgerald, lines 1152–70]

The chorus asks its questions, "Who is guilty? Who is dead? Speak!" and the messenger finally tells the news that is not news—because we in the audience know it already.

There is this same series of gestures in *Aeneid* 2, and our knowledge of the story of the fall of Troy and of the Greeks' trick with the horse serves to give the events a quality of having been inexorably fated, which in turn gives a stature to Aeneas's grief. Fitzgerald is very good here, getting the rhetorical, almost incantatory tone right. That "ruffian" in line 10 is a happy invention of his, something of a departure from the Latin *miles*, which is a neutral word for soldier. The modifier *duri* means hard, or perhaps stern, but for the internal slant rhyme in English with "Dolopian," "ruffian" is irresistible. It also splashes its meaning backward both on the Dolopians and the Myrmidons too, so there is a whipsaw effect, the retrospective insult setting up the climactic "without tears" with which the sentence ends.

Like the audiences hearing the ritual recitations of disaster in Attic tragedies, we know what is going to happen. So did Dido and her guests. There is a peculiar kind of comfort in hearing a familiar story, even if it is a terrible one. Young children demand of their parents ritualized recitations that depend on the same compact between teller and hearer, the same shared assumptions, the repetitions, and their implied verification of the world's obdurate truths.

And it is, indeed, a matter finally of what has been fated, for as Aeneas makes clear:

> Flame signals
> Shone from the command ship. Sinon, favored
> By what the gods unjustly had decreed,
> Stole out to tap the pine walls and set free
> The Danaans in the belly. Opened wide,
> The horse emitted men; gladly they dropped
> Out of the cavern, captains first, Thessandrus,
> Sthenelus and the man of iron, Ulysses;
> Hand over hand upon the rope, Acamas, Thoas,
> Neoptolemus and Prince Machaon,
> Menelaus and then the master builder,
> Epeos, who designed the horse decoy.

> [2.343–54]

Auden has observed that the poet's gold is in proper nouns. The second book of the *Iliad*, with its catalogue of the ships, is a long and boring list unless one can learn to relish the names of the men and the places. Virgil here is doing one of those show-off lists, a cadenza of specificities that are the wellspring of epic. At its most basic, it is the Word (Epos) about some deed, which is to say it is a recitation of who did what. It is told and retold, and indeed is designed to be retold. Even encountering it for the first time, we may imagine ourselves hearing a passage like this for the fifth or fiftieth, and nodding along with the speaker as the familiar names come up in the proper order. It is difficult not to do this.

It is also difficult not to respond as children do to the horrific aspect of Aeneas's story. Sinon lets the Greek soldiers out of the horse, and they kill the sentries and let their companions into the city. And then comes the carnage, but not right away. First, there is the appearance of a terrible spectre:

> That time of night it was when the first sleep,
> Gift of the gods, begins for ill mankind,
> Arriving gradually, delicious rest.
> In sleep, in dream, Hector appeared to me,
> Gaunt with sorrow, streaming tears, all torn—
> As by the violent car on his death day—
> And black with bloody dust,
> His puffed-out feet cut by the rawhide thongs.
> Ah, god, the look of him! How changed
> From that proud Hector who returned to Troy
> Wearing Achilles' armor, or that one
> Who pitched the torches on Danaan ships;
> His beard all filth, his hair matted with blood,
> Showing the wounds, the many wounds, received
> Outside his father's city walls.
>
> [2.360–74]

The one who announces Troy's fall is the dead Hector. He is the one who orders Aeneas to save himself and lays upon him the duty to save the household gods and go and dedicate to them the new walls of a new city.

What Virgil is demonstrating here is first his establishment and then his manipulation of authority. There is a combination of tone and poetic attack, a rhetorical and narrative strategy that is irresistible. What the reader already knows becomes the foundation of the story and then, to some considerable degree, its subject. Hector tells Aeneas what will happen to Troy, but then, in the next passage, the same theme is restated as Aeneas mentions, among the soldiers who fell in with him, young Coroebus, Mygdon's son.

> It happened
> That in those very days this man had come
> To Troy, aflame with passion for Cassandra,
> Bringing to Priam and the Phrygians
> A son-in-law's right hand. Unlucky one,
> To have been deaf to what his bride foretold!
>
> [2.457–62]

They are all tainted with the knowledge of their doom. "Come, let us die, / We'll make a rush into the thick of it. / The conquered have one safety: hope for none," Aeneas says (2.470–72), by which he means that they also enjoy the freedom of desperation. They go to their deaths bravely, knowing as well as we do what is going to happen, and by this peculiar stratagem Virgil puts us there with them, thus forcing us to imagine their plight which is our own—except that we can never be sure that we would have behaved so well.

Poor Coroebus doesn't last very long:

> When the gods are contrary
> They stand by no one. Here before us came
> Cassandra, Priam's virgin daughter, dragged
> By her long hair out of Minerva's shrine,
> Lifting her brilliant eyes in vain to heaven—
> Her eyes alone, as her white hands were bound.
> Coroebus, infuriated, could not bear it,
> But plunged into the midst to find his death.
>
> [2.532–39]

We think—are intended to think—of those characters in the *Iliad* who pop up, get themselves described, are brought vividly to life, and then are cut down, or impaled on spears, or dismembered. They're unlucky, like movie extras in battle scenes whose job it is to be killed. But each death is all the more affecting for the care Homer has taken with those vivifying details. There are many possible examples, but I think of Orsilochos and Krethon, the sons of Diokles, whom Aeneas kills in *Iliad* 5. Homer gives their lineage, and then says of them:

> These two as they were grown to young manhood
>   followed along with
> the Argives in their black ships to Ilion, land of good
>   horses,
> winning honor for the sons of Atreus, Agamemnon
> and Menelaos; now fulfillment of death was a darkness
>   upon them.
> These, as two young lions in the high places of the
>   mountains,
> had been raised by their mother in the dark of the
>   deep forest,
> lions which as they prey upon the cattle and the fat sheep
> lay waste the steadings where there are men, until
>   they also
> fall and are killed under the cutting bronze in the
>   men's hands;
> such were these two who beaten under the hands
>   of Aineias
> crashed now to the ground as if they were two tall
>   pine trees.
>
>   [Lattimore, 5.550–60]

Coroebus is and is not like them. Innocence and simplicity are theirs, exactly those qualities his foreknowledge—and ours—deprives him of.

There are touchstones in literature, great moments that one doesn't want to try to analyze or discuss. And the section of the *Aeneid* that follows, the description in book 2 of the fall of the city, is one of these. The purpose of poetry is not to provide students with material for exercises by which they may display their critical abilities. There is also mute awe, which is the appropriate response to the last five hundred lines of this book.

Virgil knew it was good. It is the only place where we really *like* Aeneas—and the poet so much relies on that effect having been achieved that he seldom troubles himself to prompt us toward further empathy for his hero. But Aeneas is brave and decent, human and humane here, particularly at the place where he sees:

> Lurking beyond the doorsill of the Vesta,
> In hiding, silent, in that place reserved,
> The daughter of Tyndareus. Glare of fires
> Lighted my steps this way and that, my eyes
> Glancing over the whole scene, everywhere.
> That woman, terrified of the Trojan's hate
> For the city overthrown, terrified too
> Of Danaan vengeance, her abandoned husband's
> Anger after years—Helen, that Fury
> Both to her own homeland and Troy, had gone
> To earth, a hated thing, before the altars.
> Now fires blazed up in my own spirit—
> A passion to avenge my fallen town
> And punish Helen's whorishness.
>
> [2.743–56]

He thinks of killing her, of "snuffing out a monstrous life," but then,

> at that moment, clear, before my eyes—
> Never before so clear—in a pure light
> Stepping before me, radiant through the night,
> My loving mother came: immortal, tall,
> and lovely as the lords of heaven know her.
> Catching me by the hand, she held me back,
> Then with her rose-red mouth reproved me.
>
> [2.773–79]

She reminds Aeneas that it wasn't Helen's doing but the "harsh will of the gods," and she directs him to the business of living, which is to say that he should go and look for his

father, his wife, Creusa, and his young son, Ascanius. It is a
remarkable moment, a moment of healing and of religious vision. Even with the "high masonry thrown down / Stone torn
from stone, with billowing smoke and dust," there can be
such dispensations, which do not make the disasters any the
less terrible but rather demonstrate the incalculable capacities
of the human spirit.

It is in that knowledge and with the grace we share with
Aeneas that we encounter the terrible scenes of the fall of his
city. Whatever else happens, and whatever else he does, we
think of him as an emigrant, a man who has lost his home.

We should also take note of another kind of characteris-
tically Virgilian marvel, the *allegretto pastorale* of book 8, where
Aeneas meets Evander, king of Pallentium and father of Pallas. Theirs is a studiedly simple society—the royal bedding is
a bearskin spread on strewn leaves—in which we are not required altogether to believe. The mood is fantastic—or say,
phantastic—a relief from the bloody business of warfare, and
it is reminiscent both of the pastoral life of the *Eclogues* and,
in the story of Cacus, of the mythopoetic world of the last
Georgic. The suggestion, and the appeal, are of an earlier, simpler, and better time, which Virgil contrasts with Augustan
Rome:

> He led to our Tarpeian site and Capitol,
> All golden now, in those days tangled, wild
> With underbrush—but awesome even then.
> A strangeness there filled country hearts with dread
> and made them shiver at the wood and Rock.
>
> "Some god," he said, "it is not sure what god,
> Lives in this grove, this hilltop thick with leaves.
> Arcadians think they've seen great Jove himself
> Sometimes with his right hand shaking the aegis
> To darken sky and make the storm clouds rise

Towering in turmoil. Here, too, in these walls
Long fallen down, you see what were two towns,
Monuments of the ancients. Father Janus
Founded one stronghold, Saturn the other,
Named Janiculum and Saturnia."

Conversing of such matters, going toward
Austere Evander's house, they saw his cattle
Lowing everywhere in what is now
Rome's Forum and her fashionable quarter,
Carinae. As they came up to the door,
Evander said:
                    "In victory, Hercules
Bent for this lintel, and these royal rooms
Were grand enough for him. Friend, have the courage
To care little for wealth, and shape yourself,
You too, to merit godhead. Do not come
Disdainfully into our needy home."

                                              [8.459–85]

It is a lost world, and its prospects are not good. We know
that Evander's son, Pallas, is going to die, because we can spot
ironies when we see them. And Evander's farewell to his son,
when Pallas goes off the next day with Aeneas, is all too clear:

"But O high masters, and thou, Jupiter,
Supreme ruler of gods, pity, I beg,
The Arcadian king, and hear a father's prayer:
If by thy will my son survives, and fate
Spares him, and if I live to see him still,
To meet him yet again, I pray for life;
There is no trouble I cannot endure.
But, Fortune, if you threaten some black day,
Now, now, let me break off my bitter life
While all's in doubt, while hope of what's to come
Remains uncertain, while I hold you here,
Dear boy, my late delight, my only one—

And may no graver message ever come
To wound my ears."
                         These were the father's words,
Poured out in final parting. He collapsed
Completely, and the servants helped him in.

[8.776–92]

We know that Pallas is a goner, and that Evander will hear
the gravest of all possible messages, and it is, in considerable
measure, our knowingness that separates his simpler and
purer world from ours. Its loss, the loss of an Eden, a paradise,
a barely remembered childhood, our own and the world's, is
the cost of Aeneas's project. And his sad silence before the
poor old man is ours too.

The conclusion of book 8 is devoted to the description of
the making of the shield for Aeneas by Vulcan at Venus's re-
quest, and then to a set-piece description of the shield itself.
Homer's shield of Achilles is one of the great set pieces of the
Iliad, and Virgil used the occasion to find a way of praising
Augustus and the peace he had established.

Vivid in the center were the bronze-beaked
Ships and the fight at sea off Actium.
Here you could see Leucata all alive
With ships maneuvering, sea glowing gold,
Augustus Caesar leading into battle
Italians, with both senators and people,
Household gods and great gods: there he stood
High on the stem, and from his blessed brow
Twin flames gushed upward, while his crest revealed
His father's star.

[8.911–21]

Auden likes Homer's shield better, as I think I do too, for its
brooding consideration of the worlds of war and peace, or of
contemplation and action. Auden, in "The Shield of Achilles,"
could see the grief for

A plain without a feature, bare and brown,
No blade of grass, no sign of neighborhood,
Nothing to eat and nowhere to sit down,
Yet congregated on its blankness, stood
An unintelligible multitude,
A million eyes, a million boots in line,
Without expression, waiting for a sign.

If Virgil's shield suggests any such grief, it does so only by indirection. What he is celebrating is Augustus's triumph at the battle of Actium and the end of savagery, or at least its interruption. While there is no obvious irony, I think it would not have surprised Virgil to learn that the tranquility of Augustus was only temporary—but it was all the more precious for that, and it remains all the worse a comment on the affairs of most men of most times that if such intervals are actually possible, we mostly fail to realize them.

If he was wonderfully wise in the *Eclogues* and the *Georgics,* he had by no means lost his wits or his clear vision. We now read these passages of praise for the emperor with some uneasiness, knowing how random a thing peace is and how long the odds are against wise government, but this seems truly and properly Virgilian in its mood. The note in Homer is clearer, but the grief implicit in Virgil's description is almost as profound and moving.

DIDO'S SHADOW

She rof hirselve to the herte,
And deyde thorgh the wounde smerte.
And al the maner how she deyde,
And alle the wordes that she seyde,
Whoso to knowe hit hath purpos,
Rede Virgile in Eneydos
Or the Epistle of Ovyde,
What that she wrot or that she dyde;

And nere hyt to long to endyte,
Be God, I wolde hyt here write.
—Chaucer, "The House of Fame,"
lines 373–82

Over the first four books, which is to say the first third of
the *Aeneid*, Dido presides. She is not only much more attractive but, at least on the surface, more interesting than Aeneas.
Her predicament—and Virgil's vivid depiction of it—is indeed so appealing as to put the structure of the whole poem
at risk, as surely as the attractiveness of Lucifer comes close
to throwing *Paradise Lost* out of kilter. Dido is the character in
Latin literature who was immediately successful—she appears only a few years later in Ovid's *Heroides* in much the
guise she is to retain for the following couple of millennia.

Ovid considers the unreasonableness of Aeneas's behavior and, in an imaginary letter from Dido to her lover, is quite
explicit:

'Tis then resolv'd poor *Dido* must be left,
Of Life, of Honour, and of Love bereft!
While you, with loosen'd Sails, & Vows, prepare
To seek a Land that flies the Searchers care.
Nor can my rising Tow'rs your flight restrain,
Nor my new Empire, offer'd you in vain.
Built Walls you shun, unbuilt you seek; that Land
is yet to Conquer; but you this Command.
Suppose you Landed where your wish design'd,
Think what Reception Forreiners would find.
What People is so void of common sence
To Vote Succession from a Native Prince?
Yet there new Scepters and new Loves you seek;
New Vows to plight, and plighted Vows to break.
When will your Tow'rs the height of *Carthage* know?
Or when, your Eyes discern such Crowds below?
If such a Town and Subjects you could see,

Still wou'd you want a Wife who lov'd like me.
For, oh, I burn, like Fires with Incense bright:
Not holy Tapers flame with purer Light:
Aeneas is my Thoughts perpetual Theme;
Their daily Longing, and their nightly Dream.
Yet he ungrateful and obdurate still:
Fool that I am to place my Heart so ill!
     ["Dido to Aeneas," trans. John Dryden, lines 7–30]

She persists this way into the Western tradition for sentimental and probably un-Virgilian reasons—she is beautiful
and loving and doomed. For the tender-hearted, this is
enough to give her that special charm of members of endan-
gered species, staring out at us from the posters at zoos to
criticize our heartless and reckless way of life. Aeneas, in this
analogy, is on the side of progress, history, industrialization,
and jobs. Such people are successful, maybe even correct and
justifiable, but less immediately endearing.

On the other hand, a more stern and realistic appraisal of
Aeneas's behavior—which is admittedly and even defiantly
irrational—involves a comparison with Abraham, whose willingness to sacrifice Isaac is at least as repellent and uncongenial, but which is, nonetheless, the test to which God (or
gods, or the fates, or history) puts him. He behaved differently from the way we would have done, but that may be because he was Abraham and we aren't.

One could also suggest that the dramatic purpose of
Aeneas's recitation in book 2 of the details of the fall of Troy
is to provide a motivation for Dido's passion for Aeneas. She
makes this connection herself:

How princely, how courageous, what a soldier.
I can believe him in the line of gods,
And this is no delusion. Tell-tale fear
Betrays inferior souls. What scenes of war
Fought to the bitter end he pictured for us!
What buffetings awaited him at sea!

> Had I not set my face against remarriage
> After my first love died and failed me, left me
> Barren and bereaved—and sick to death
> At the mere thought of torch and bridal bed—
> I could perhaps give way in this one case
> To frailty.
>
> [4.16–26]

What Aeneas feels for Dido is not otherwise explained—perhaps because it would be impossible for Virgil to explain it. Perhaps he felt such an explanation was unnecessary. The job Aeneas has been given by Fate is to go to Italy and to found Rome. "He came to Italy by destiny," says Virgil, right at the beginning. We know this and Aeneas knows it too. But having been blown off course by a storm, he makes a landfall at Carthage and allows himself to tarry there with Dido, and he forgets himself entirely and either positively misleads Dido or, at the very least, fails to correct her belief that he has given up this nonsense about founding a country and is now content to settle down in Carthage. We never know what, if anything, is going on in Aeneas's mind.

But then, why should he treat her differently? She is a Carthaginian, remember—which is to say a queen of the city that was Rome's enemy. She is a Madama Butterfly—actually, Puccini modeled Butterfly on Purcell's Dido. As a women from the East—a Tyrian by birth—she is likely to have suggested to Roman readers another vamp of more recent vintage, the one who had been on the wrong side at the battle of Actium—the Egyptian queen and Antonius's companion, Cleopatra.

These are perhaps unattractive considerations, almost rude remarks, but they may not be incongruous with the intention of the poem. One fundamental distinction between the Homeric epics and Virgil's adaptation of the form for patriotic purposes, I should think, would be their different senses of ethnic and national difference. The thrust of the *Aeneid* is to make a connection between the Romans and the Trojans, to claim the Trojan heroes as the Romans' forebears. The Homeric assumptions and intentions were quite different. As Gregory Nagy suggests in *The Best of the Achaeans*, part of Homer's purpose was to weld the various Greek communities and settlements into one unified and harmonious culture, resolving local enmities and rivalries into an overarching system based on heroism and honor. Enemies were therefore equals, and the glory of the Greek victory came from the valor and honor of the Trojans they had defeated. There are many moving moments in the *Iliad*, but none is more effective and affecting than that in which Priam

> sat huddled
> at the feet of Achilleus and wept close for
>   manslaughtering Hektor
> and Achilleus wept now for his own father, now again
> for Patroklos. The sound of their mourning moved in the
>   house. Then
> when great Achilleus had taken full satisfaction in sorrow
> and the passion for it had gone from his mind and
>   body, thereafter
> he rose from his chair, and took the old man by the
>   hand, and set him
> on his feet again, in pity for the grey head and the
>   grey beard,
> and spoke to him and addressed him in winged words.
>   [Lattimore, 24.509–17]

There can be no clearer statement imaginable of Homer's inclusion of the Trojans among the ranks of humankind. The basic machinery of the *Iliad* depends on that moral equivalence between Greek and Trojan and their comparable weight and value as human beings. The death of Achilles, which is the climax of the poem, the focus toward which every line and gesture have been pointing, is never shown. What we have, instead, are glimpses of what it would be like—what it will be like—as it impends all the time over the action. We see Patroklos go out to fight in Achilles' armor, and Patroklos's death and funeral therefore prefigure those of Achilles. And here now that Hector lies dead, we see Achilles again making the connections clear for the readers and hearers. If these two men are weeping together, and if Achilles weeps for his own father, then Priam is also weeping in part for the death of Achilles. If the weeping is for Patroklos, then it is also in part for Achilles.

The nobility is not limited to Achilles, either. He is a willing enough pupil, but King Priam is the instructor who has spoken with both moral and dramatic authority:

> Honor then the gods, Achilleus, and take pity upon me
> remembering your father, yet am I still more pitiful;
> I have gone through what no other mortal on earth
>   has gone through;
> I put my lips to the hands of the man who has killed
>   my children.
>
> [24.503–06]

It is a moment both terrible and splendid, and our sympathies flow all the more abundantly because there is no attempt to channel them. The death of Hector is, of course, an occasion for grief, as the death of Achilles will be. Indeed, it has been suggested that in the Homeric poems, the gods are relatively frivolous creatures, of no weight or substance precisely because they are immortal. They do not bleed blood but mere ichor. The humans are the ones who can die and who therefore carry a moral weight. Theirs are the choices that matter and they are capable of tragedy—as the gods can never be. Longinus has said of Homer that "he made his gods men, and his men gods," and surely it is our fraternity as "mortals" that Homer celebrates, relies on for his effects, and assumes in the hearts of a generous audience.

Whether through temperamental differences or, more probably, because of the differences in their political intentions, Virgil seems less cosmopolitan in his sympathies. His purpose after all was the celebration of Augustus, Rome, and peace. In Dryden's words, "He concluded it to be in the interest of his country to be so governed; to infuse an aweful respect into the people towards such a prince; by that respect to confirm their obedience to him, and by that obedience to make them happy. This was the moral of his divine poem."

Early on in book 1, Jupiter confirms Aeneas's destiny:

> In Italy he will fight a massive war,
> Beat down fierce armies, then for the people there
> Establish city walls and a way of life.
> When the Rutulians are subdued he'll pass
> Three summers of command in Latium,
> Three years of winter quarters. But the boy,
> Ascanius, to whom the name of Iulus
> Now is added—Ilus while Ilium stood—
> Will hold the power for all of thirty years,
> Great rings of wheeling months. He will transfer
> His capital from Lavinium and make
> A fortress, Alba Longa. Three full centuries
> That kingdom will be ruled by Hector's race,
> Until the queen and priestess, Ilia,
> Pregnant by Mars, will bear twin sons to him.
> Afterward, happy in the tawny pelt
> His nurse, the she-wolf wears, young Romulus
> Will take the leadership, build walls of Mars,
> And call by his own name his people Romans.
> For these I set no limits, world or time,
> But make the gift of empire without end.

[1.355–75]

This is not merely a celebration of a national tradition but of a blood-line. And on occasion in the course of his praise of the Romans, Virgil is willing to dispraise others, to deprecate those with whom there are no connections of race and kinship. In Virgil's account of the fall of Troy, one prominent fig-

ure is Sinon, the liar who persuades the Trojans that it is
essential for them to take the horse into the city. And once the
Greek soldiers are out of the horse and at large in the town,
they are comic figures, mistaking enemies for friends and only
victorious because they have superiority in numbers.

> Danaans from all sides
> Rallied and attacked us: fiery Ajax,
> Atreus' sons, Dolopians in a mass—
> As, when a cyclone breaks, conflicting winds
> Will come together, Westwind, Southwind, Eastwind
> Riding high out of the Dawnland; forests
> Bend and roar, and raging all in spume
> Nereus with his trident churns the deep.
>
> [2.546–53]

Sex and death are the two basic things in poetry as in life.
And in sex as in battle, the status of the Greeks seems like that
of the Tyrian/Carthaginian Dido—which is to say not quite
human. Therefore, when Aeneas is tarrying there with her, it
doesn't even cross his mind that he may be violating some
ethical principle or law of hospitality. The furthest Virgil goes
in making excuses for Aeneas is to give us the dramatic moment at the beginning of book 5 in which, having put to sea,
he looks back

> Upon the city far astern, now bright
> With poor Elissa's pyre. What caused that blaze
> Remained unknown to watchers out at sea,
> But what they knew of a great love profaned
> In anguish, and a desperate woman's nerve,
> Led every Trojan heart into foreboding.
>
> [5.4–9]

Elissa, of course, is another name for Dido. Aeneas can only
guess, as he has always guessed, at what she has done,
thought, or felt.

Oddly enough—or maybe not so oddly—the Dido epi-

sode has proven so successful as to have taken off from the
Aeneid. Dido's character took on its own independent existence and survived, as no other figure of Latin literature was
able to manage, into European literature. She figures promi-
nently in Chaucer's "House of Fame":

> But let us speke of Eneas,
> How he betrayed hir, allas!
> And lefte hir ful unkyndely.
> So when she saw al utterly
> That he wolde hir of trouthe fayle,
> And wende fro hir to Itayle,
> She gan to wring hir hondes two.
> "Allas!" quod she, "what me ys woo!
> Allas! is every man thus trewe,
> That every yer wolde have a newe,
> Yf hit so longe tyme dure,
> Or elles three, peraventure?"
>   [lines 293–304]

She appears as well in Marlowe's play, and in the Purcell and
the Berlioz operas, but with that important difference that she
is invariably the heroine and represents the openness and self-
lessness of women, while Aeneas is the cad representing the
faithlessness of men. The notion of Romantic Love had of
course intervened to re-energize the story and give it a rather
different purpose from that which Virgil had intended—but
Virgil is lucky that way, with Christianity or Romantic Love
coming along to revive his work and reputation.

Dr. Johnson's remark about patriotism being "the last refuge of a scoundrel" has proved to be more than a piece of imp-
ish wit, and we have to keep reminding ourselves that the
ideal of Rome was not so limited, that the imperium was in-
clusive and its aim was a kind of peace and order among the
various peoples within the empire.

But still, but still. . . .

In the *Aeneid*, Dido is a figure representing aliens and losers. She is a Carthaginian whose dying prayer is a defiance not only of her individual betrayer, Aeneas, but of Rome itself and therefore of the Augustan ideal of world harmony and reason. She is very clear:

> "This I implore,
> This is my last cry, as my last blood flows.
> Then, O my Tyrians, besiege with hate
> His progeny and all his race to come:
> Make this your offering to my dust. No love,
> No pact must be between our peoples; No,
> But rise up from my bones, avenging spirit!
> Harry with fire and sword the Dardan countrymen
> Now, or hereafter, at whatever time
> The strength will be afforded. Coast with coast
> In conflict I implore, and sea with sea,
> And arms with arms: may they contend in war,
> Themselves and all the children of their children!"
>
> [4.863–75]

Aeneas, we are to allow, may have been a bit louche, but this is extreme! The Punic Wars start right here! Aeneas is the epic's hero after all, and if he has unbent and unbuttoned himself rather more than he should have, Jupiter sends his messenger, Mercury, to remind him of his destiny:

> "What have you in mind? What hope, wasting your days
> In Libya? If future history's glories
> Do not affect you, if you will not strive
> For your own honor, think of Ascanius,
> Think of the expectations of your heir,
> Iulus, to whom the Italian realm, the land
> of Rome are due."
>   And Mercury, as he spoke,
> Departed from the visual field of mortals
> To a great distance, ebbed in subtle air.
> Amazed, and shocked to the bottom of his soul

By what his eyes had seen, Aeneas felt
His hackles rise, his voice choke in his throat.
As the sharp admonition and command
From heaven had shaken him awake, he now
Burned only to be gone, to leave that land
Of the sweet life behind. What can he do? How tell
The impassioned queen and hope to win her over?
What opening shall he choose?

[4.369–87]

Actually, Fitzgerald is being kinder to Dido here than Virgil was. His "impassioned" is a rather sympathetic rendering of *furentem*, which suggests "raving." (Mandelbaum gives us "frenzied," and Day-Lewis, a bit bizarrely, "temperamental.") Virgil's suggestion is clearly that she was a Tyrian to start with, and has now become a raving Tyrian, which is to say she is even further removed from the realm of the human. Aeneas has loftier matters to attend to—the founding of Rome, the rights of his heir. Dido's *furor* is awkward and distressing, a mere momentary tactical problem, and one which, we must observe, he does not solve with much grace. His blatantly nonheroic tactic is just to sneak away.

There is one final observation to make about this rather unflattering depiction of Aeneas. Virgil's model here is the *Odyssey*. Book 4 of the *Aeneid* follows upon a very Odyssean book 3, and Dido is more nearly equivalent to Nausicaa than to Calypso or Circe, if only in that she is a mortal. Odysseus tells the Phaeacians the stories of his wanderings just as Aeneas narrates his stories—of the fall of Troy, from the Trojan point of view of course, and of his wanderings—to Dido. There is an erotic element in Odysseus's encounter (in book 6 of the *Odyssey*) with Nausicaa: he is naked when they meet, and her servants flee in embarrassment. And Athena makes Odysseus invisible in book 7 as he makes his way to the palace, just as Venus makes Aeneas invisible on his way to Carthage. But Odysseus does not seduce Nausicaa. Instead, he treats her and her father with honor.

Aeneas behaves quite differently and, unless we assume Virgil to have been a total moron, there has to be some purpose to his curious series of actions, some rhetorical explanation that would reverse the disastrous effect of the hero's conduct and show it in a different light. The death of Dido may be one more burden Aeneas has to carry, another grief, and if my view is correct of the Pergamene mathematics of the victims' suffering as the measure of the victors' glory, then Dido's pain and death are the pedestal for a heroic figure of Augustus we are continually invited to imagine.

It is possible to forgive, or at least forget, injuries we have suffered from others; the injuries we have inflicted are the ones we dwell on for years, even forever. The strategy of the exposition is to keep us in Dido's head. We know what she thinks but have to suppose what Aeneas may be thinking, and we must decide whether or not to allow him the shame we might feel ourselves in such a sorry circumstance. It seems that Virgil has calculated this perspective, taking considerable pains to ensure that our view of the event is from the angle and at the distance he has contrived. At the opening of book 5, he has Aeneas and the sailors looking back at the flames, and while the sight is alarming and "led every Trojan heart into foreboding," we do not know what Aeneas is thinking. He is left a blank—it is a Gary Cooper or Humphrey Bogart blankness, one of those faces that is a map of any quality of experience we choose to read into its weathered lines. And if we allow that Aeneas is a man of destiny, a man with a mission, then that mission's cost is to be reckoned according to the value we put on his sense of guilt and shame—which turns out to be considerable, as we learn in book 6, in what seems to me one of the great moments of the poem.

The venture into Hades was an epic convention and the occasion for the prophecy of the coming of Augustus and the Roman Empire. But it was also an inviting occasion for other kinds of visionary Virgilian flight. It is a nightmare realm, quite different from Homer's:

Now voices crying loud were heard at once—
The souls of infants wailing. At the door
Of the sweet life they were to have no part in,
Torn from the breast, a black day took them off
And drowned them all in bitter death.

[6.575–80]

And into this much more vivid and tormented version of an
underworld, Aeneas ventures, and of course he sees Dido:

The Trojan captain paused nearby and knew
Her dim form in the dark, as one who sees,
Early in the month, or thinks to have seen, the moon
Rising through cloud, all dim. He wept and spoke
Tenderly to her:
                              "Dido, so forlorn,
The story then that came to me was true,
That you were out of life, had met your end
By your own hand. Was I, was I the cause?
I swear by heaven's stars, by the high gods,
By any certainty below the earth,
I left your land against my will, my queen.
The gods' commands drove me to do their will,
As now they drive me through this world of shades,
These mouldy waste lands and these depths of night.
And I could not believe that I would hurt you
So terribly by going. Wait a little.
Do not leave my sight.
Am I someone to flee from? The last word
Destiny lets me say to you is this."
Aeneas with such pleas tried to placate
The burning soul, savagely glaring back,
And tears came to his eyes. But she had turned
With gaze fixed on the ground as he spoke on,
Her face no more affected than if she were
Immobile granite or Marpesian stone.
At length she flung away from him and fled,

His enemy still, into the shadowy grove
Where he whose bride she once had been, Sychaeus,
Joined in her sorrows and returned her love.
Aeneas still gazed after her in tears,
Shaken by her ill fate and pitying her.

[6.608–39]

Without question, he is sorry. And also without question, it
does no good. The glow of that pyre is still searing in "the
burning soul, savagely glaring back." After this moment, we
cannot doubt that his inclination may have been to stay, that
he would have stayed but for his sense of mission. The only
question left is whether that conviction of destiny and mission
is insane or actual. And the evidence we have in the fora of
Rome, the temples and the buildings of Rome, is that Aeneas
was not delusionary. There are the proud buildings one can
still touch, solid, stolid, of "immobile granite or Marpesian
stone."

The fundamental difference between the victors and the
vanquished is one that raises another question, of course. The
belief in fate, or at least Virgil's recourse to the convention of
that belief, is a basic element in the construction of the poem.
It is upon that belief or convention that the conduct of Aeneas
can be explained, in regard to Dido or to anything else he
does. The course of events seems to have been decided in ad-
vance, already determined by *fatum*, and while men and the
gods may endeavor to intervene or delay or modify, the broad
outlines of what must happen seem to have been predeter-
mined.

It is possible to try to make sense of this system, but the
results have not been noticeably successful, perhaps because
the enterprise is a misguided one. Gordon Williams has con-
sidered one such attempt, Cyril Bailey's *Religion in Virgil*
(1935), and rightly judges it to be a well-meaning muddle. Williams's own view in *Technique and Ideas in the "Aeneid"* is that

techniques *are* ideas, and that "if there is religious conviction as such expressed in the *Aeneid* (and it is far from clear that there is), it is certainly not to be found displayed on the surface of the text." Williams reminds us that Virgil was not writing a religious tract but a poem, and that it is therefore to the narrative and aesthetic consequences of fate and the gods that we ought to pay attention, asking how Virgil uses these figures to foreshadow, to highlight, and, most important, to make his figures cast the long and stately shadows the epic requires. In that modest and practical manner, we can begin to read properly the dimension of fate in the work.

It seems to me that the main trick of the *Aeneid* is a juggling with time, the construction of the poem requiring that we look back not only from our time but from Augustus's and Virgil's time to the twelfth century B.C. What we must first recognize is that we enjoy, from this peculiar vantage point, a striking play of enormous shadows on very distant walls. Everything Aeneas does projects across a millennium and more, and while that magnification gives the hero a considerable stature, it costs him in definition. That scantiness of detail we may sometimes notice may be the result not of Virgil's inattention (or incompetence) but of the peculiarity of his grand strategy. The comparison we ought to make is, again, with Milton, whose attempt in *Paradise Lost* to give us a homey item or two in a domestic scene before the Fall produced one of the funniest lines in the poem. Raphael has dropped in on Adam and Eve in their bower, and Milton feels obliged to tell us:

> Raised of grassy turf
> Their table was, and mossy seats had round,
> And on her ample square from side to side
> All autumn piled, though spring and autumn here
> Danced hand in hand. A while discourse they hold;
> No fear lest dinner cool; when thus began
> Our Author.

> [V.391–97]

James Holly Hanford's famous note on these lines is worth citing: "This reminder of the social convenience of an uncooked banquet has excited laughter among the irreverent. But Milton wants to interest us in all the speculations, literal and otherwise, about Eden, as he himself was interested."

Maybe so, but one must always vote with the irreverent unless the poet gives good reason not to. Milton, of course, was consciously modeling his work on the *Aeneid*—both poems are in twelve books, and they both strike the modern reader as rather official in tone and address, like post office, museum, and old-fashioned railroad station architecture. But Milton's interest in the specifics of prelapsarian housekeeping is a gaffe, a violation of the tone of the piece at which irreverent laughter is quite correct. Virgil rarely makes that kind of mistake.

If we must look beyond the work of art, it is not to philosophy and religion that we should turn but to the tropes of ordinary speech for clues to an understanding of the meaning of fate. Too close an examination will only destroy fragile constructions that were never meant to bear scrutiny—but we employ such figures all the time, and they are not altogether without significance. At the least, a sense of history and even of fate is what we attribute to moments—often meetings or partings—of particular importance, moments that have changed our lives. To say that something was "fated" is not necessarily to insist on predestination but only to assert that one's life, and indeed the world, would not be recognizable or even imaginable otherwise.

The Marxist idea of the dialectic of history—with its suggestion of an inevitable set of calculable reactions (that produce, eventually, a dictatorship of the proletariat)—is simply a rhetorical inflation of the ordinary sense we have that some incidents are important. This feeling is decked out with some Hegelian window dressing in order to secularize what would otherwise be an intolerably theological reading of the process

of the world's events. Virgil uses the notion of fate in this ordinary and common-sense way—to suggest a distinction between the unimportant things most of us do most of the time
and the occasionally significant, resonant, consequential action most of us engage in only rarely but that heroes and
leaders experience more frequently, either because of their positions in life or through their characters. Aeneas not only
functions at that level, he exists there. This is his natural hab-
itat, which is why it would have been a fundamental error to
make reference to the temperature of his lunch. The tricks of
time are the smoke, and the conventions of the gods and destiny are the mirrors by which this effect is achieved. Aeneas
may not, in the long run, be likable or even interesting, but
what Virgil does with him is all one can imagine a poet doing.

It is in that simple dramatic sense that I take some of the
business about fate, in Virgil's practice. That Dido is unaware
of the significance or the possible consequences of her encounter with Aeneas is made clear by the messenger from Jupiter who comes to ensure a friendly reception for the hero.

> . . . he sent the son of Maia down
> from his high place to make the land of Carthage,
> The new-built town, receptive to the Trojans,
> Not to allow Queen Dido, all unknowing
> As to the fated future, to exclude them.
>
> [1.399–403]

To put more weight on the foreordained future is to wreck the
poem, for if Dido is going to die, and Carthage is going to fall,
if Troy was going to fall, and nothing Aeneas could have done
would have changed any of this, there is nothing interesting
for us to watch except perhaps the intricacy with which the
automata are engineered.

But the gods do know and, more to the point, we know
what is going to happen. Or, to put it in a more practical way,
the gods know because we know. And we know because we
have read this or heard this before. Even in Virgil's time, the

story of Aeneas was familiar material. Its familiarity was exactly what attracted him. If he was to construct a heroic work
that praised Aeneas and Augustus, it had to be on familiar
and conventional themes. And in these circumstances, the
gods represent us, knowing what we know about the outcomes. Aeneas, himself, is not quite so sure, but his faith in
the prophecies and his willingness to sacrifice comfort and
safety and even, as far as we know, love for the abstraction of
Rome's destiny is what makes him (let us admit it) annoying,
but also (let us admit this too) great.

   Consider one of the famous cruces of the poem. In their
last interview, Dido, beside herself with grief and rage, tells
Aeneas:

> "If divine justice counts for anything,
> I hope and pray that on some grinding reef
> Midway at sea you'll drink your punishment
> And call and call on Dido's name!
> From far away I shall come after you
> With my black fires, and when cold death has parted
> Body from soul I shall be everywhere
> A shade to haunt you! You will pay for this,
> Unconscionable! I shall hear! The news will reach me
> Even among the lowest of the dead."
> At this abruptly she broke off and ran
> In sickness from his sight and the light of day,
> Leaving him at a loss, alarmed, and mute
> With all he meant to say. The maids in waiting
> Caught her as she swooned and carried her
> To bed in her marble chamber.
>   Duty-bound,
> Aeneas, though he struggled with desire
> to calm and comfort her in all her pain,
> To speak to her and turn her mind from grief,
> And though he sighed his heart out, shaken still
> With love of her, yet took the course heaven gave him

And went back to the fleet. Then with a will
The Teucrians fell to work and launched the ships.

[4.529–52]

Fitzgerald is quite right here to have given us not so much
the Latin as a gloss on the Latin. The crucial phrase is "at pius
Aeneas," and R. D. Williams's view in *The Aeneid of Virgil* is
one that Fitzgerald very clearly shared:

> Some commentators have here failed to understand the
> significance Virgil has put into the use of the epithet.
> Page, for example, says Virgil " begins the next paragraph
> quite placidly *at pius Aeneas* . . . ! How the man who wrote
> the lines placed in Dido's mouth could immediately after-
> wards speak of 'the good Aeneas etc.' is one of the puz-
> zles of literature." But the only possible defense for
> Aeneas' actions is his *pietas;* in any other capacity than as
> a man of destiny he should have stayed—*pietas* is why he
> must leave, and Virgil wants us to remember this. It may
> be that many (presumably including Page) would wish
> that *pietas* had not prevailed, but it is utterly wrong to
> object to being told that it has done so. We might translate
> "But Aeneas, because of duty. . . ."

"Duty-bound" is even better. We can, with poor Page,
dislike his being duty-bound. Most of us can even admit—or
boast—that in Aeneas's place, we should behave differently,
stay, and say, "To hell with destiny and Rome!"
    More likely than not, Virgil expects such a reaction and
relies on it. How else can we calculate the weight of Aeneas's
burden?
    I think the moment is one to which Virgil devoted partic-
ular care and attention. Aeneas here wants to comfort Dido's
pains with words, "dictis avertere curas," but he cannot. His
silence here is the set-up for the larger and even emptier one
we shall experience in his encounter in the underworld. It is
paid off when Dido turns away from him in silence.

AENEAS IN THE UNDERWORLD

Mi aunty's baby still. The dumbstruck mother.
The mirror, tortoise-shell–like celluloid
held to it, passed from one hand to another.
No babble, blubber, breath. The glass won't cloud.

The best clock's only wound for layings out
so the stillness isn't tapped at by its ticks.
The settee's shapeless underneath its shroud.

My mind moves upon silence and *Aeneid* VI.
                      —from "Study" by Tony Harrison

It is a working-class death in Leeds in the twentieth century, and the poet, in an oppressive room, distanced from
his family and feeling guilty about it, feeling therefore the
pain of separation along with that of bereavement (his uncle
has died), turns in desperation to some soothing and noble
notion of how it ought to be. He tries to supply—for himself
and for the scene—something of the dignity that ought to
attach to such a moment, and he turns, of course, to the very
thing that has separated him from his family, his education
and what it can offer, which is "*Aeneid* VI."

Which is quite a lot, actually, one of the great passages
of literature, stately and yet humane, not so lugubrious as to
be grotesque or macabre, but clear enough in its suggestion
of a spooky otherworld which is a necessary part of the Virgilian suggestion of inevitability and fate that is at the heart
of the epic. We are, here, at the half-way point. This is the
keystone of the structure.

Aeneas arrives in Italy, disembarks, climbs the hill to
Apollo's temple, and consults the Sibyl at Cumae, whose
appearance is quite wonderful in the root sense of the word:

The priestess called them to her lofty shrine.
The cliff's huge flank is honeycombed, cut out
In a cavern perforated a hundred times,
Having a hundred mouths, with rushing voices
Carrying the responses of the Sibyl.
Here, as the men approached the entrance way,
The Sibyl cried out:
                    "Now is the time to ask
Your destinies!"
                    And then:
                                "The god! Look there!
The god!"
                    And as she spoke neither her face
Nor hue went untransformed, nor did her hair
Stay neatly bound: her breast heaved, her wild heart
grew large with passion. Taller to their eyes
And sounding now no longer like a mortal
Since she had felt the god's power breathing near,
She cried:
                    "Slow, are you, in your vows and prayers?
Trojan Aeneas, are you slow? Be quick,
The great mouths of the god's house, thunderstruck,
Will never open till you pray."
                                        Her lips
Closed tight on this. A chill ran through the bones
of the tough Teucrians.

                                        [6.65–90]

She predicts the war in Italy and, when he asks to be
guided to the underworld to see Anchises, his father, she
explains how he will be permitted to descend if he finds a
golden bough that is hidden in a nearby wood. He sees to
the burial of one of his comrades and then goes after the
golden bough, which is his token of admission to (and pass
for his return from) Hades.

What is past and what is to come are the limits of the present, and therefore the limits of reasonable action. The past is unchangeable and the future unknowable. The presentation of the underworld—better than Homer's—implies something spacious and mysterious about how things happen in the world, which is to say about fate:

> Before the entrance, in the jaws of Orcus,
> Grief and avenging Cares have made their beds,
> And pale Diseases and sad Age are there,
> And Dread, and Hunger that sways men to crime,
> And sordid Want—in shapes to affright the eyes—
> And Death and Toil and Death's own brother, Sleep,
> and the mind's evil joys; on the door sill
> Death-bringing War, and iron cubicles
> of the Eumenidës, and raving Discord,
> Viperish hair bound up in gory bands.
> In the courtyard a shadowy giant elm
> Spreads ancient boughs, her ancient arms where
>   dreams,
> False dreams, the old tale goes, beneath each leaf
> Cling and are numberless.
>
> [6.376–89]

He reaches Acheron, is ferried across, passing the souls of the unburied—among whom he sees Palinurus, the pilot, to whom he promises a performance of the proper rites. Aeneas and the Sibyl cross the Styx and she drugs Cerberus so they can pass.

And then. . . . But no summary can do this justice. One must read for oneself the ascending series of encounters and revelations, resonant and impressive, marvelously designed and calculated. There are the souls of those who died as infants, and those who died falsely accused, and the souls of suicides. There are those who died of unrequited love, Phaedra and . . . Dido! (He begs forgiveness but she turns away without speaking to rejoin her husband, Sychaeus.) Aeneas and the Sibyl come to the famous warriors, and Priam's son Deiphobus recounts how he was murdered on the night of the fall of Troy by Menelaus, with the help of Helen (whom he, Deiphobus, had married after Paris was killed). At last they reach the Elysian Fields where the blessed dwell, and Anchises greets Aeneas, tells him more about how the underworld works, and then reveals to him the destiny that awaits their line—Rome's founding and growth, and greatness, and, eventually, the reign of Augustus.

Emperor Augustus was Virgil's patron and his epic's subject. Anchises, giving Aeneas a look into the future, tells him:

> Turn your two eyes
> This way and see this people, your own Romans.
> Here is Caesar, and all the line of Iulus,
> All who shall one day pass under the dome
> Of the great sky: this is the man, this one,
> Of whom so often you have heard the promise,
> Caesar Augustus, son of the deified,
> Who shall bring once again an Age of Gold
> To Latium, to the land where Saturn reigned
> In early times. He will extend his power,
> Over far territories north and south
> Of the zodiacal stars, the solar way,
> Where Atlas, heaven-bearing, on his shoulders
> Turns the night-sphere, studded with burning stars.
> [6.1058–71]

This is the structural foundation of the entire undertaking.

Quintilian set the canon, which held through the empire and was later on received as authoritative by the Renaissance: "As Homer provided an auspicious opening for my Greek list, so Virgil does for the Latin, for he is without doubt second only to Homer in all epic, Greek or Latin. I shall apply the words I heard in my youth from Domitius Afer. When I asked him what poet he would place next to Homer he replied, 'Virgil is second, but much nearer first than third.' We must indeed yield to Homer's superhuman and celestial stature, but Virgil shows greater application and precision, perhaps because his was the harder task. For Homer's unrivaled flights we may find Virgil's uniform excellence an adequate balance. All others follow at a greater interval" (*Institutio oratoria* 10.1.85–86).

One result of such a judgment is to be seen in those poignant papyri that have been found in Graeco-Roman Egypt, of the *Aeneid* marked up with an interlinear translation into Greek—for these were young Hellenes, boning up for the competitive exams they had to take for civil service jobs. It is easy to bridle at a poem so many people have encountered under such circumstances. And it would be disingenuous to deny that the poem appears to us under this huge cloud. For in being so official a poem, while it has enjoyed certain advantages, it has also taken on corresponding liabilities. Augustus's rule was tranquil enough, but Nero and Caligula were to some extent implied by that degree of centralization of power. After Julius Caesar, the course of government might conceivably have returned to some version of a republic, but after the battle of Actium and fifty years of Augustus's regime, there was nobody left who could remember the Republic and, even worse, no one who believed in its idea.

It may be that the genius of Rome was for empire anyway. It has been suggested that Greek is a language of liberty and Latin one of power. That formulation is too clever and neat but not altogether wrong. One thinks particularly of the way in which Latin verbs crack their whips to order the foregoing elements of their sentences and, after some considerable suspense—which some Freudian critics have seen as a kind of aggression—declare at last a meaning. Be that as it may, we are inescapably children of the twentieth century, are less innocent than most of mankind, and ought at least to have learned from the shambles of our time to be suspicious of dictators and worry about their propagandists.

There has been an attempt to get round this difficulty by turning Virgil into a kind of Shostakovich to Augustus's Stalin. The *Aeneid*, according to this reading, is actually an anti-Augustan document, a subversive performance in which subtext takes away much of what the surface is giving. The idea is that Aeneas is rather a clod, uninteresting and even repellent, an oxlike hero who plods through the poem with no particular reason to keep going other than that it is "fated" (and his name happens to be on the title page). The really appealing characters are in the opposition—Dido in the first half of the epic, and Turnus in the second.

It is a plausible reading to which, in some ways, I am drawn, but we must be careful not to overstate or oversimplify the case. The surface of the verse is not contorted at all and its stance is too positive and suave to give us any reason to question Virgil's *bona fides*. There is a recognition of the limits of the hero and, by extension, the limits of the Augustan and imperial ideal, but from this allowance for the complications of history, politics, and morals, we cannot leap to the subversive and partisan messages some twentieth-century liberals would prefer to find in the poem. The official Virgil was almost certainly the real Virgil, and it was probably his intention to celebrate Rome and Augustus as well as he could—the only limits being those of his own talent and temperament, and of course the truth. There is a melancholy cast to Virgil's basic sensibility which is almost sufficient to account for some of the curious idiosyncrasies of his great work. (In what other heroic poem does the hero make his first appearance with the announcement that he wishes he were dead?) And to give legitimacy and even modishness to his own aesthetic and emotional preferences, there was, as Philip Hardie suggests (in *Virgil's* Aeneid: *Cosmos and Imperium* [Clarendon Press, Oxford, 1986]), a convenient and congenial style, the Pergamene "Hellenic Baroque" which provided Virgil with exactly those opportunities he needed for the expression of gloom and the sense of *lacrimae rerum.*

This style is best known from the statue of the "Dying Gaul" (it used to be known, incorrectly, as the "Dying Gladiator"). Work in this mode is sinuous and expressive, and its usual subject is the sufferings of the defeated. Instead of glorious representations of the victors' triumphs or of their struggles and exploits that proved eventually to be successful, the artists who worked in this style chose to depict the dramatic agonies of the defeated—from which the scope and extent of the victory could be inferred. At its worst, these pieces look a little as if their creators were gloating over the plight of the losers, but what saves them is their surface, the craftsmanship that puts those sufferings at a certain aesthetic distance, so that there is a generalization and abstraction in their significance. Yes, the "Dying Gaul," and the "Gaul and his Dead Wife" are pitiable, but Pergamon's own ruin—which we can see now, either on the ruined hill in Turkey or in the museum in Berlin where many of its artifacts are on display—is anticipated, or at least allowed for, in the melancholy assertion that all things that are made can be unmade, the suggestion that polished surfaces are only waiting to be broken by time and chance.

That kind of deep gloom is a part of the *Aeneid.* I suggest that the fundamental drama of the poem is the tension between private pessimism and public optimism. Yes, he seems to say, it's a good time we've been having, but how long can it last? From the dramaturgic point of view, there are problems of tact Virgil had to face. Except for the catastrophe of book 2 and the fall of Troy, which Aeneas survives, he is a winner, a victor, after all. His is a success story, and the difficulty, therefore, is to keep him sympathetic. In the *Iliad,* even though the Greeks are to win, the story's hero is Achilles, whose death is to be a part of that victory. The general direction of that poem is from rage to death, a re-

lentless downward motion that we see figured over and over
again in the battle scenes, with each vividly depicted casualty
a miniature epic. In the *Odyssey*, the motion is exactly contrary and Odysseus is victorious as he emerges from the
nonbeing of Calypso's island to the life of Ithaca. The pattern
of the *Odyssey* is not unlike that of some Japanese samurai
movies in which the hero is insulted, aggrieved, and injured
for most of the film until, in a spasm of righteous rage and
more or less supernatural skill, he extracts payment from the
malefactors in a spectacular bloodbath. Odysseus's losses are
considerable—of his entire crew he is the only survivor, and
at home there are those rapacious suitors trying to take his
place on his throne and in his bed. His struggle is to return
home for a restoration of the *status quo ante*, and his sufferings
are in some ways akin to the trials of Job. Aeneas, however,
is moving from Troy to a destiny in Italy where he is fated
to found a nation. He has his sufferings too, in the loss of
his wife and of Troy. But neither Dido nor Turnus has anything to do with the fall of Troy, nor are they in any sense
equivalents of the Laestrygonians or the Cyclops. They are
innocent and even admirable, the aggrieved parties, and it is
Aeneas who is the intruder.

What Virgil does to keep him from being an utter embarrassment is to weight him with as much burden of suffering and of family piety as he can contrive. Aeneas's father,
Anchises, is riding on his son's shoulders—literally so at one
point. And while Virgil is staking a claim for his poem as a
part of the Homeric epic cycle by having Aeneas relate, in
book 2, the fall of Troy, he is also allowing Aeneas his best
moments. He is, nonetheless, a difficult hero to like. When
we meet him, he wants to die; and when we take our leave
of him, he has just slain the noble Turnus in an action which
may be fated but is still arbitrary and even whimsical. Virgil
makes it clear that this last death is entirely unnecessary:

> Fierce under arms, Aeneas
> Looked to and fro, and towered, and stayed his hand

Upon the sword-hilt. Moment by moment now
What Turnus said began to bring him round
From indecision. Then to his glance appeared
the accurst swordbelt surmounting Turnus' shoulder,
Shining with its familiar studs—the strap
Young Pallas wore when Turnus wounded him
And left him dead upon the field; now Turnus
Bore that enemy token on his shoulder—
Enemy still. For when the sight came home to him,
Aeneas raged at the relic of his anguish
Worn by this man as trophy. Blazing up
And terrible in his anger, he called out:

"You in your plunder, torn from one of mine,
Shall I be robbed of you? This wound will come
From Pallas: Pallas makes this offering
And from your criminal blood exacts his due."
He sank his blade in fury in Turnus' chest.
Then all the body slackened in death's chill,
And with a groan for that indignity
His spirit fled into the gloom below.

[12.1277–98]

It is an extraordinary and peculiar ending to an epic: as
if Aeneas, having won, is no longer interesting. Virgil no
longer makes any perfunctory gesture in the direction of re-
taining our sympathies for Aeneas. Turnus has asked—albeit
without much real hope—for *missio*, but while we would sig-
nal for the victim's life, Aeneas sees Pallas's swordbelt and
strikes. Virgil's eyes—and ours—turn away from Aeneas to
follow Turnus's disappearing spirit, which is the last image
of the poem. The light of the epic is that of Dido's pyre, as
its gloom is that into which Turnus's shade flees! Small wonder, then, that many intelligent and sensitive readers have
read the work as signifying some contrary, subversive, and

perhaps anti-Augustan tendencies in Virgil. There is, un-
doubtedly, some mordant suggestion here, but it is up to
each of us to decide how sentimental or clear-eyed to be
about it, or what in particular Virgil might have meant. It
seems sufficient, to me, to take the ending as a sign of
Aeneas's descent from the lofty realm of epic hero to the
lower and less immaculate domain of practical kingship. Actual kings and warriors do, indeed, make decisions in the
heat of battle and the press of business that are arbitrary and
flawed. We cannot be naive about how the world works.

I think, in this connection, of the objections ultra-ortho-
dox Jews made to the establishment of the state of Israel by
political action—because they believed that would mean the
Jews had descended from their purely spiritual plane (waiting patiently for God and the Messiah) to the practical questions of government and statecraft. That position has always
seemed to me crazy but perhaps correct. And I see in the
end of the *Aeneid* some such complicated nexus of meanings,
which are all the more convincing because they are complicated.

It is not necessary to extrapolate from that sad and almost bitter ending any equation between Aeneas and Augustus or any implied criticism of Augustus's regime, and
without such compulsion we ought to look first at the possibility that the poem means what it says, and assume Virgil
to have been an honest workman, performing under the
terms of his commission to produce an epic for emperor and
empire. That he produced what was taken to be an official
poem is a matter of historical record.

The revelations of Anchises to Aeneas, the coming at-
tractions of the history of Rome, build to what we suppose
will be their climax as Anchises prophesies the eventual appearance of Augustus. But he goes on from there, and the
last figure to appear is Marcellus, Augustus's nephew, adopted

son-in-law, and designated heir, whose death was the death of the emperor's dynastic hopes.

At the very least, this passage is peculiar. Auden makes fun of it in his poem "Secondary Epic," wondering why the revelation "Should so abruptly, mysteriously stop, / What cause could he show why he didn't foresee / The future beyond 31 B.C., / Why a curtain of darkness should finally drop." It's a puzzler, all right, and if that last joke about 31 B.C. is too easy, the "No, Virgil, no" with which the poem begins is appropriate, authoritative, and properly regretful.

The politics of succession is always a ticklish subject. In Robert Graves's version, which, if it isn't strictly correct, ought to be, Tiberius waits more or less patiently while Livia and her servants poison any possible rivals who don't have the good fortune to get killed on a battlefield somewhere. There are some readers of the *Aeneid* who see in the curious placement of Marcellus's death as the last of the prophecies of Anchises a proleptic suggestion of the collapse not only of Augustus's dreams but of the whole decline and fall of Rome. It is also typically Virgilian to find a minor chord with which to end his cadenza. On its surface, it is a condolence note to Augustus, but it is surely more than that. If Augustus is a creature of special grace—a vessel of Rome's fate, a god— then it is a disturbing thing to see his fondest hope dashed by larger and darker forces. For him to suffer a loss is for Rome to suffer the loss of his invulnerability. History has not stopped. This is not the perfection to which all the past has tended. More things will happen, vicissitudes await, the wheel of Fortuna continues to turn—and while this may be a comfort in terrible times, it is a disturbing thought in moments of prosperity and tranquility.

The mention here of Marcellus is an odd gesture which, if we judge it to have been successful, would be comparable in its tact and intricacy to Dryden's daring "Ode to the Pious Memory of the Accomplisht Young Lady, Mrs. Anne Killigrew, Excellent in the Two Sister-Arts of Poesie and Paint-

ing." The Dryden piece is wacky but it does work and is a
model of modulation as the poet first establishes the abstract
dedication to the arts as his topic and then descends to the
subject at hand, the admittedly modest accomplishments of
this young woman who has recently died. Dryden's is an
impressive demonstration of generosity and tact that nonetheless respects the limitations of his subject's achievements.

Virgil, it seems to me, is similarly successful. It takes a
while to get used to it, but the implication is clear enough.
There are some people who choose to see it simply as another
in the series of deaths of young men, cut off in their prime
by history's rough and clumsy hands. Virgil often connects
his images so that they accumulate and exchange their energies, and it is possible to relate the death of Marcellus to
that of Menoetes, for instance, the Arcadian who hates war
but who is nonetheless killed by Turnus in book 12.

Well, perhaps, but Augustus is at least a member of the
poem's putative audience, sitting in the imperial box at the
end of the horseshoe. (According to Suetonius, this imperial
presence was more than putative: Virgil actually recited this
book to Augustus and his household, and Octavia is said to
have fainted at the Marcellus passage.) Whether that tradition is true or not, we have a sense that Virgil is bending the
poem here in order to pay an extravagant compliment to the
imperial family, while at the same time warning us that all
men are mortal—even Augustus—and that we should prepare ourselves for less agreeable circumstances.

When people bridle at the *Aeneid* and call it an imperialist
poem, this is what they are talking about:

>   "Oh, do not ask
> About this huge grief of your people, son.
> Fate will give earth only a glimpse of him,
> Not let the boy live on. Lords of the sky,
> You thought the majesty of Rome too great
> If it had kept these gifts. How many groans

Will be sent up from that great Field of Mars
To Mars' proud city, and what sad rites you'll see,
Tiber, as you flow past the new-built tomb.
Never will any boy of Ilian race
Exalt his Latin forefathers with promise
Equal to his; never will Romulus' land
Take pride like this in any of her sons.
Weep for his faithful heart, his old-world honor,
His sword arm never beaten down! No enemy
Could have come through a clash with him unhurt,
Whether this soldier went on foot or rode,
digging his spurs into a lathered mount."

[6.1179–96]

And so on.

What they fail to understand is that Augustus's loss is a shared one, and that the real losers are those who believed too much or relied too greatly on the idea that Rome's destiny had been accomplished with the permanence of all those marble buildings that were so imposing.

There is also the puzzling tradition of Virgil's deathbed instruction that the poem should be burnt. Was it only a persnickety dislike of having a less than perfect piece released to the world? There are inconsistencies, famous irrationalities (Aeneas, for instance, meets Palinurus in Hades only one day after his pilot has fallen overboard, but Palinurus's version of the event mentions an impossible three-day swim before he is set upon by the nasty locals, who kill him for his rags.) There are half-lines, fragments that Virgil presumably intended to finish at some later date. So it is possible that he was thinking only of such small details. But it is also conceivable that he was, at the end, disgusted by the tendency of the whole poem and that he realized in a melodramatic moment of deathbed clarity how he had misspent the dozen years he is said to have labored on this piece.

The reverse is also possible, for it has been suggested

that what Virgil regretted was that he had been insufficiently grateful to Augustus for the kindness the emperor had shown him in his last illness. Even if the poem were some sort of disguised attack on Augustus, it cannot be excluded that Virgil may have repented at the last of his criticism. But there is no end to such analyses. With no evidence to go on—or to limit speculation—we can also suppose if we wish that the gesture was an intentionally empty one, that Virgil knew his executors and that he relied on them to ignore this last request he had made only to wriggle out of any responsibility for what the poem said (either in praise or in criticism of Augustus).

I think of the *Eclogues* and *Georgics* as more than enough to justify Virgil's eminence in the Western tradition. (Indeed, that is one more reason for my ambivalence about the *Aeneid*—that the epic has rather hogged the stage.) Still, the historical importance of the *Aeneid* is such that no civilized person should be deprived of that poem. It is there, looming over the literary landscape and casting a shadow each of us must come to terms with. Of how many works of the imagination can such a thing be said? And in the end, having lived with it for a while, one comes to see that it has to be the way it is, given the world it addresses. It is a sad stern poem, that could not be otherwise.

What Virgil might as easily have demanded, then, on his deathbed, was that the world be burnt—except that he wasn't crazy.

THE FUNERAL GAMES: NISUS AND EURYALUS

The first half of the *Aeneid* is often called the Odyssean half, because it describes a journey and includes a visit to the underworld. The second half, which is, in this scheme, the Iliadic half, involves a war, this time on Italian soil, and this time one in which Aeneas is inevitably victorious. A war poem inevitably involves a series of battle scenes from the tumult of which the artist must either discover some order, or on which he must try to impose some comprehensible pattern—or he may deliberately refuse to do either. In *War and Peace* and *The Red and the Black*, both Tolstoy and Stendhal make their subversive suggestions that there is no order whatever in battle, that the encounter is fundamentally chaotic, that even the generals have only an imperfect notion of what is going on, while individual participants are even less well informed.

That may be the accurate view, but it is not Virgil's. He has either beguiled himself into some belief in the machinery of history and fate, or, more probably, he is simply following Homer here in trying to impose some poetic form upon the flux of these encounters on the field. The chances of battle are the chances of the world, and it is at least logically possible to suppose that some rationale governs them; what is surprising is that Virgil finds his rationale not so much in the broad historical determinations of the gods and Fortuna as in the bondings and pairings of companions and enemies.

He is also following Homer in his description, in book 5, of the funeral games. Virgil offers a series of comic turns to which many readers respond with some combination of puzzlement and exasperation. Between the death of Dido at the end of book 4 and the death of Palinurus at the end of book 5, there is a series of races and boxing and shooting matches that are not only nondramatic but even antidramatic. In the *Iliad*, the games in book 23 follow immediately upon Patroklos's funeral and its bizarrely primitive, all but savage rites, which include human sacrifice—there are twelve Trojan youths that Achilles "put to the sword, as he willed their evil hour." The funeral rites are for Patroklos, but also for Achilles himself, inasmuch as Patroklos has come to Achilles in a dream to ask to be inurned with Achilles' remains, in the same vessel together. Hector has just been killed and his body is lying there unburied, so the rites, insofar as they have been denied him, also concern him. And the games, coming as they do in the midst of all that death, are a peculiarly effective celebration of life.

Aeneas's games in book 5 are for the anniversary of the death of Anchises, which is a rather less pressing and immediate occasion. Their comic quality is curious: Virgil is not a natural comedian. One can understand those readers who are put off by the preppiness of the games. It is as if those masters from the classics building had changed into sweatsuits and jogged out onto the playing fields with peaked caps on their heads and silver whistles hanging from their necks on fancy lanyards, eager to impose upon us with a whole new set of arbitrary demands.

The events, moreover, are silly, so shamelessly rigged as to make the most hardened Hollywood hacks cover their faces. In Homer, the games are an occasion for us to see demonstrations of characteristics of figures who are already familiar. The poem is drawing to its close and Diomedes, Agamemnon, Menelaus, Aias, and Odysseus are hardly strangers at this point. But Virgil is introducing characters in these games, and their performances are set-ups for pay-offs that will come later on. There are rather heavy-handed directorial touches by which Virgil attempts to keep our interest from flagging as he constructs this machinery for effects he has in mind for further down the road. To make a reasonable judgment about the games in book 5, then, we must consider the ways in which these peculiar constructions are intended to work.

On a purely thematic level, there is a consistency in these games that we do not find in Homer, an order almost too insistent and obvious, in which the sporting events are a figuring of a death. The book begins with the flames of Dido's pyre observed from shipboard and ends with Palinurus falling overboard. The first of these sporting events is the rowers' race in which Gyas, one of the captains, tosses his too cautious helmsman, Menoetes, overboard and takes the tiller himself. It is presented as a funny scene:

> When heavy old Menoetes
> Slowly at last emerged from the sea bottom

Drenched and streaming, up he climbed and sat
Atop the dry ledge. Trojans had laughed to see
His plunge, his swimming, and now laughed again
As he coughed up sea water from his chest.

[5.233–38]

But that the comic plunge must be preparatory to Palinurus's much more serious one, we can hardly doubt. There is
the figure of the dove to which Virgil keeps referring. He
brings it up first in the boat race:

Mnestheus meanwhile, more ardent for his luck,
With his fast oars in line, the wind behind him,
Took the shoreward leg through open water.
As a wild dove when startled into flight
Beats her affrighted way over the fields—
A dove whose cote and tender nestlings lie
In a rock cranny—with fast clapping wings,
But soon in quiet air goes floating on
With wings extended motionless: just so
Mnestheus, just so the Seabeast cleft the sea,
Running for the home stretch, and just so
She glided, borne by her own impetus.

[5.271–82]

We see the dove again, in the shooting match, where it
is the target. This is the same kind of match as we see in Homer, but in Virgil's treatment of the material there is a twist
in that the first arrow severs the flaxen cord by which the dove
is tied to the post; the second arrow kills the dove; and the
third bursts into flame in a supernatural augury. The dove's
death, moreover, is rather curiously described:

Down she plummeted
And left her life in the upper air of stars,
But brought down with her the transfixing shaft.

[5.665–67]

That contrary motion, that assertion of upwardness and

then downwardness, is exactly what Virgil uses to character-
ize Palinurus's fall overboard at the end of the book:

> Somnus leaned over him and flung him down
> In the clear water, breaking off with him
> A segment of the stern and steering oar.
> Headfirst he went down, calling in vain on friends.
> The god himself took flight into thin air.
>
> [5.1122–28]

It is impossible as a coincidence. The direction of each of
the athletic events is downward, death-ward. The boat race
has Menoetes' immersion. The boxing match ends with a figuring of a human sacrifice when Entellus, the old champion,
having beaten Darës, receiving the palm and the prize bul-
lock,

> Glorying in his courage and his prize,
> Spoke out:
>   "Son of the goddess, Teucrians all,
> Now see what power was in me in my prime,
> And see the death from which you rescued Darës."
> He set himself to face the bull that stood there,
> Prize of the battle, then drew back his right
> And from his full height lashed his hard glove out
> Between the horns. The impact smashed the skull
> And fragmented the brains. Down went the ox
> Aquiver to sprawl dying on the ground.
> The man stood over it and in deep tones
> Proclaimed:
>   "Here is a better life in place of Darës,
> Eryx; here I lay down my gauntlets and my art."
>
> [5.613–27]

The only event that does not end in the clear figuring of
a death is the footrace in which Nisus and Euryalus make their
appearance. Much as Aias in the *Iliad* slips in ox dung, Nisus
slips in gore from the sacrificed animals, staggers, and pitches

headlong into the mire. Out of contention himself, he trips
Salius in order to insure that Euryalus, his beloved, may take
first prize. It doesn't seem exactly sporting, although it is, so
far as I can determine, the only place where Aeneas actually
laughs (or at least smiles—*risit*, line 358). As it turns out, however, Joe Paterno, the football coach at Penn State, found the
Aeneid inspiriting and instructive—he devotes a chapter of his
autobiography, *Paterno* (Random House, 1989), to his encounter in parochial school with Virgil. I yield to his superior authority.

The notion of sport as a moral and spiritual arena is not
absurd. Paul Weiss talks about sport in a philosophical way
(in *Sport: A Philosophic Inquiry* [Southern Illinois University
Press, 1969]) and considers its significance as a display of human excellence. Homer and Virgil discuss sport, but Aristotle
did not, and therefore it has not been part of the philosophical
curriculum. One wants to quarrel with Virgil not that he
spends time describing these games but that his descriptions
are so dim. What can it mean for Nisus, having tripped in the
gore, to deliberately foul Salius, the second-place guy, so that
Euryalus (Nisus's lover!) should win?

The claims of patriotism are all very well, and the *Aeneid*
is a celebration of emperor and empire, but in Virgil's heart
and, more important, at the core of his fundamental poetic
practice, such abstract claims turn out to be remote and in-
substantial. What Virgil finally appeals to is the bedrock of
friendship and love—of whatever kind and quality. The sortie
in book 9 in which Nisus and Euryalus return is the more serious restatement of what Virgil has figured in the footrace in
book 5. At the start of the battle scene, Ascanius offers Nisus
incentives that are actually prizes—as if the mortal enterprise
were another athletic event:

> two cups well shaped in silver,
> Rough with embossing, that my father took
> The day Arisba fell; twin tripods, too,

> Two gold bars and an ancient winebowl, gift
> Of Dido the Sidonian. . . .
>
> [9.370–74)

It isn't Nisus who answers Ascanius but Euryalus, and he doesn't even refer to these proffered prizes. Instead, he asks that in the event of his death, Ascanius should look after his mother—to whom he does not have the heart to bid farewell and whose tears he could not endure.

The terms of the offer are those of the playing field. The terms of the reply are those of fate, for we are all sophisticated enough to guess that if a character is talking about his death, the chances of his surviving the encounter are not good. This foreshadowing technique has become a convention in war movies and westerns because it is efficient and plausible, allowing as it does for whatever degree of foreknowledge we want to attribute to the speaker. Doomed or not, off they go to get word to Aeneas, and rather irrelevantly—it wrecks their mission, after all—they hack their way through a fair number of Rutulian extras. They are almost successful in their effort, have "put the camp behind them" and are "making for safety" when they are cut off by the cavalry, a troop of "horsemen three hundred strong, all bearing shields, / With Volcens in command." These horsemen see the gleam of moonlight on the helmet Euryalus had lifted from Messapus. Like the crack of a twig in Cooper's woods, the helmet gives Euryalus away and the horsemen surround him. Nisus, however, manages to escape:

> But all at once, he stopped and looked around
> In vain for his lost friend.
>
> "Euryalus,
> Poor fellow, where did I lose you? Where shall I
> Hunt for you?"
>
> [9.549–53]

No, no! Don't do it! But we know, from the footrace, what
has to happen. And of course it does:

> Backward in his tracks
> As he recalled them, now he went, and strayed
> Through silent undergrowth. He heard the horses,
> Heard the clamor and calls of the pursuit,
> And after no long interval a cry
> Came to his ears: Euryalus now he saw
> Set upon by the whole troop—first undone
> By darkness and the treacherous terrain,
> Now overwhelmed by the sudden rush of men
> Who dragged him off, though right and left he strove.
> Now what could Nisus do? What strength had he,
> What weapons could he dare a rescue with?
> Should he then launch himself straight at the foe,
> Through many wounds hastening heroic death?
>
> [9.555–68]

We know the answer to that question. Euryalus knows it
too. But Nisus, ignorant still, prays to the moon—the very
moon whose light betrayed them in the first place—to guide
his weapon. The first javelin is accurate enough and kills
Sulmo. And a second javelin kills Tagus. But there are three
hundred horsemen here, let us remember, and their patience
is by now wearing thin. Volcens has already captured Euryalus, and as he goes to dispatch him,

> Mad with terror, Nisus cried aloud.
> He could not hide in darkness any longer,
> Could not bear his anguish any longer:
> "No, me! Me! Here I am! I did it! Take
> Your swords to me, Rutulians. All the trickery
> Was mine."
>
> [9.602–07]

It does no good. Volcens stabs Euryalus, and Nisus
plunges ahead in a frenzy and kills Volcens,

Even as he died himself. Pierced everywhere,
he pitched down on the body of his friend
And there at last in the peace of death grew still.

[9.630–32]

The language is more than suggestive. It is a perfect gay love-death, a pagan version of the martyrdom of Saint Sebastian with all those arrows piercing everywhere and an exquisite look of rapture on the face.

Whatever it was that bound Achilles and Patroklos—who are clearly Virgil's models—binds Nisus and Euryalus. Beyond this Homeric precedent, though, there is a Virgilian pattern that extends throughout the entire *Aeneid*. What is supposed to be an epic celebrating the abstract value of patriotism hinges upon the most personal and intimately concrete connections, as if in countervalence to the poem's declared purpose. Aeneas leaves Dido not only for fate and destiny but because he owes his first allegiance to his son, whom he would otherwise be depriving of an empire. Pallas becomes a kind of foster son, an alternate Ascanius, and when Pallas is killed, Aeneas exacts vengeance at the end of the poem by killing Turnus.

The machinery is perhaps cumbersome, but its purpose is all the more clearly defined by the great pains Virgil has taken to achieve the effects he wants. Ascanius can't be killed—otherwise there is no Rome to descend from Aeneas. Therefore, Virgil has to work with the complicated algebra of equivalence by which Aeneas's exaction from Turnus of payment in blood is as personal a reparation as Nisus's passionate and suicidal exaction of blood payment from Volcens.

To be musical and not excessively fanciful, the footrace incident is the subdominant chord; the sortie in book 9 is the dominant chord; and the death of Turnus is the tonic to which the other musical notes have been an inexorable progression. In the *Iliad*, Aias slips in cow shit. Virgil's alteration is not whimsical. Nisus slips in blood.

These personal bonds of blood or affection are also the basis of the actions of the opponents, the Latins and Rutulians. The impression I have is that in recognizing in Turnus and Mezentius such concerns with loyalty and honor, Virgil was praising them, or at least recognizing them as moral equals of the Trojans. It was a ticklish business to describe the war against the Italians without giving offense to those Italians who were now a part of the Empire and to whom Roman citizenship had been extended in the relatively recent past. For that matter, a number of important Romans were Italians—Maecenas was an Etruscan and even Tiberius was a Claudian of Sabine stock. The Marsic (or Italian) War had been fought from 91 to 88 B.C., only eighteen years before Virgil's birth and fifty years or so before he wrote the *Aeneid*. The Italians, therefore, could not be treated with disrespect, which is what Virgil carefully avoided. Even "harsh Mezentius," the Etruscan "who held the gods in scorn" and who comes closest to the conventional villain, is given a moment of magnificence at the end of book 10 when he dies fighting to avenge the death of his son, Lausus:

<blockquote>
Aeneas on the run
Came up, pulling his sword out of the sheath,
Stood over him and said:
                "Where is the fierce
Mezentius now, and his bloodthirsty soul?"
The Etruscan with his eyes cast up regained
His senses, drinking in the air of heaven.
</blockquote>

[10.1254–60]

The question is rhetorical in form, but the answer is more complicated than anything Aeneas might expect, for Mezentius is redeemed, has regained his senses, raises his eyes and his sights, and drinks in the air of heaven. Once more, Aeneas actually looks bad, and Mezentius is quite correct in his reply:

<blockquote>
"Bitter as gall, my enemy,
Why pillory me and hold up death before me?
</blockquote>

Taking my life you do no wrong; I had
No other expectation, coming to battle.
Lausus, my son, made no compact with you
That you should spare me. One request I'll make
If conquered enemies may ask a favor:
Let my body be hid in earth. I know
On every hand the hatred of my people.
Fend off their fury and allow me room
In the same grave with my son."

[10.1261–72]

The scene prefigures that at the end of the poem in which
Aeneas kills Turnus, but it also looks backward to Nisus and
Euryalus, for Mezentius is no longer a tyrant here but only a
loving father who has been wounded, who has come to the
engagement to die, moved by his grief at the loss of Lausus,
who was "unexcelled in beauty / Except by Turnus of the Lau-
rentines." It is in aid of Lausus that Turnus comes to kill Pallas
(10.671ff.), for which action he will later pay with his own life.
Saved by Turnus, Lausus comes to the aid of his father, whom
Aeneas has wounded in the groin with a spear throw.

Lausus "groaned at the sight for love of his dear father /
And down his cheeks the tears rolled" (10.1109–10). Mezentius is carried to safety, but Aeneas kills Lausus, whose body
is carried to Mezentius.

Mezentius' heart knew well for whom they wept
When still far off. Gouging up dust he soiled
His white hair, spread his hands to heaven; and when
The body came, he clung to it.
                                    "Did such pleasure
In being alive enthrall me, son, that I
Allowed you whom I sired to take my place
Before the enemy sword? Am I, your father,
Saved by your wounds, by your death do I live?
Ai! Now at the end exile is misery to me,
Now the wound of it goes deep! There's more:

My son, I stained your name with wickedness—
Driven out as I was, under a cloud,
From throne and scepter of my ancestors.
Long since, I owed my land, my hating folk,
Punishment for my sins. I should have given
My guilty life up, suffering every death.
I live still. Not yet have I taken leave
Of men and daylight. But I will."
                                        At this
He stood up on his anguished thigh, and though
Strength ebbing and the deep wound made him slow,
Undaunted he commanded that they bring
His mount, his pride and stay, on which he rode
From all his wars victorious.
                                        [10.1180–1204]

What Euryalus's mother cannot do, Mezentius can. He
and Aeneas fight and Aeneas triumphs, but not at all sport-
ingly. It is not a pretty kill. Aeneas kills Mezentius's horse,
and Mezentius is trapped under the animal. In this position,
he plays Priam to ask for his own body's burial. Aeneas's response is curiously absent, as Virgil keeps the focus of attention on the defeated Etruscan:

                                        This said, he faced
With open eyes the sword's edge at his throat
And poured his life out on his armored breast
In waves of blood.
                                        [10.1273–76]

Aeneas is hardly even in the scene, except as the unseen hand
at the other end of that sword. Mezentius is not passive but
grammatically and dramatically active as he pours out his life
in blood upon his armor.

On the Italian side, there are the Latins, the Etruscans,
the Rutulians . . . and Ruritanians and Freedonians? It is difficult to keep them straight, not because the lines of alliance
and enmity are so complicated but because, in the long run,

Virgil doesn't really want us to. The quarrels and ties that seem to count are personal ones. The death of a friend, or the breaking of an engagement (Turnus is engaged to Lavinia, the daughter of the Latin king, but her father decides that she is to marry Aeneas instead)—these are the promptings of the action. The fact that Mezentius is cruel enough to have provoked an insurrection among his Etruscan subjects is virtually irrelevant here, for while Virgil supplies us with this information, he makes no dramatic use of it. We get, instead, a loving father, grief-stricken, wounded—in the groin, of course —not only willing to face death but positively welcoming it.

The athletic competitions conclude with an archery contest modeled on Homer's, but with the difference that the last shot bursts into flame and turns into an omen or at least a literary icon—for we have left the natural world behind and are well into the realms of religious belief and poetic technique. The reader is at any rate alerted to any arrows that may be fired from this point onward. And, indeed, there is a whole quiver full of such arrows. Iulus kills the tame stag to start the war (7.654–728). Diana's sentinel, Opis, punishes Arruns for killing Camilla:

> The hands aligned, the left hand felt the point,
> The right hand, and taut bowstring, touched her breast.
> All in one instant Arruns heard the arrow
> Whistle in the ripped air and the arrowhead
> Thud in his body. As he moaned and died
> His fellow troopers rode off, unaware,
> And left him in the dust, a spot unknown
> On the wide terrain. Opis, taking wing,
> Went soaring to the high Olympian air.
>
> [11.1171–79]

There is also, in Fitzgerald's version, Venus's "quivering flash" in book 8 (line 712) to mark the compact of Aeneas and Evander and the fact that that king has committed his son,

Pallas, to Aeneas's care. It is a lovely notion, tactfully referring as it does to the arrows, but that suggestion of archery is not in the Latin "vibratus." Indeed, Virgil is less than tactful here in the archery event, and he intrudes authorially to turn the poem for a moment into its own footnote:

> But here before their startled eyes appeared
> an omen of great import: afterward
> Mighty events made it all clear, and poets
> Far in the future fabled it in awe.
>
> [5.672–75]

Or one poet, anyway. Aeneas awards Acastes, whose arrow it was, first prize, recognizing him as Jupiter's chosen one.

Finally, there is the performance of the children, their equestrian maneuvers and mock battle. Iulus (i.e., Ascanius) is the leader of one of the three troops, and once again Virgil is insistent on pointing out to even the most obtuse reader the significance of what is going on:

> The column split apart
> As files in the three squadrons all in line
> Turned away, cantering left and right; recalled,
> They wheeled and dipped their lances for a charge.
> They entered then on parades and counter-parades,
> The two detachments, matched in the arena,
> Winding in and out of one another,
> And whipped into sham cavalry skirmishes
> By baring backs in flight, then whirling round
> With leveled points, then patching up a truce
> And riding side by side.
>
> [5.749–59]

It is impossible not to realize that these sham skirmishes will turn bloody very soon. Indeed, there is so much foreshadowing in these games and so much display of architectural purpose that their surface shows the stress. My guess is that Virgil laid some of this in rather late in the composition of the poem, going back to this book to fiddle with the material after he had written much of the rest of the work. That might account for one of the peculiar inconsistencies attentive readers have spotted—Euryalus and Nisus are introduced here in the footrace, and then, in book 9, Virgil introduces them again, as if they haven't already been established and their destinies indicated. One possible explanation is that, when Virgil wrote the introductory passage in book 9, the footrace hadn't yet occurred to him. It certainly reads as though two new characters are making an entrance:

> Nisus guarded a gate—a man-at-arms
> With a fighting heart, Hyrtacus' son. The huntress
> Ida had sent him to Aeneas' side,
> A quick hand with a javelin and arrows.
> Euryalus was his comrade, handsomer
> Than any other soldier of Aeneas
> Wearing the Trojan gear: a boy whose cheek
> Bore though unshaven manhood's early down.
> One love united them, and side by side
> They encountered combat.
>
> [9.241–50]

It seems unlikely for it to have slipped Virgil's mind that Nisus and Euryalus have already been introduced. It is more plausible to suppose that Virgil wrote this episode in book 9 and then went back to the funeral games in book 5 to revise that footrace, perhaps substituting these two for a couple of other runners and intending eventually to emend or delete what had now become a redundant and unnecessary gesture of presentation in the later passage. In any event, there is evidence of calculation and contrivance of an effect that is part of the basic Virgilian repertoire—the probable aim of which is to convert a sequential narrative into something more than a series of happenings and to make events resonate and echo. Virgil wants us to recognize a tendency in these events and eventually to allow them as manifestations of destiny. The epic mode is one of destiny, which depends not so much on the meddling of the gods and Fortuna as on a poetic and dramaturgic engineering. Aeneas, Dido, Turnus, Pallas, Mezentius, Nisus, Euryalus, and the rest of them are all characters, not merely of Virgil's imagination but of what we take to be the stage of history.

These pairings and adumbrations are the means by which Virgil engineers that height he needs to make those figures loom with their ominous and marvelous shadows.

THE ENDING WITH TURNUS

In the last four books of the *Aeneid*, the action is not only predictable but inevitable. Considering the constraint under which Virgil was working, having painted himself into this very narrow corner, what is surprising and impressive is that the poem is not a total disaster. In fact, book 12 is one of its best and most effective pieces.

The bold stroke Virgil relies on to achieve a dramatic tension that the logic of the poem ought to have precluded is his presentation of Turnus, Aeneas's chief opponent and the main obstacle to his purpose. Turnus is going to be defeated and killed—we know this. What we might not have expected is that Virgil makes him sympathetic, even heroic, and not merely as a foil for Aeneas but in his own right. One could argue that in the *Iliad* Hector is a more likable fellow than Achilles. Hector, the married man with a wife and kid, doesn't sulk in his tent as Achilles does. He has no such luxury. The Trojans, after all, are the defenders against the attack of the Achaeans. In Paris's abduction of Helen, and even in Priam's decision to keep Helen in Troy, Hector played no part. He is blameless, has done nothing to provoke this war, but never complains, doing his duty and giving his life in defense of his city. In comparison, Achilles is rather a prima donna, glorious and grand despite his often shabby and insubordinate behavior.

In the *Aeneid*, Turnus is an antagonist quite different not only from Hector but, as far as I can see, from any previous character in literature. In Turnus, what Virgil has invented, millennia before Rousseau and Chateaubriand dreamed it up, is the idea of the noble savage. Turnus is the *primitif* we are invited to admire and yet to whom we can also in some measure condescend. History and politics may have had some weight in Virgil's calculation of this dramatic strategy, which flattered the Romans (Aeneas, their man, is victorious) while it avoided offending the Italians who had only recently been incorporated into the empire (Turnus, their man, loses but looks good doing so). It is primarily for the dramatic advantage, however, that Virgil must have excogitated this remarkable figure. The inevitability of Aeneas's triumph is clear by the end of book 8 and, with four books to go, he found in Turnus an invaluable vehicle for our interest and sympathies. The drama of the last third of the poem is not so much on the page as in the heads and hearts of the readers when we find that we are investing ourselves in Turnus.

His undoing may be a matter of destiny, but he shares responsibility and collaborates in his ruin, attaining the grandeur and paying the price of tragic stature, for he demonstrates as clearly as Oedipus a fatal flaw of character. In Oedipus, that flaw is arrogance or hubris; in Turnus, rashness.

Turnus does what primitives do, acting without calculation and demonstrating a spontaneity that, to a sophisticate like Virgil, must have seemed both enviable and poignant. And Virgil flatters his readers by including us in his salon, in which the directness and the passion of a Turnus is exotic, expensive, and therefore even enviable—as it is also, of course, regrettable. Turnus is not unlike Othello, another *primitif* who is both greater and lesser than his Venetian masters. The motif of the Rutulian hero is frenzy: he is *amens, turbidus, fervidus, ardens, furens,* and *trepidans. Insania, furor,* and *violentia* are his hallmarks, as W. A. Camps points out in *An*

Introduction to Virgil's Aeneid (Oxford University Press, 1969).
The *violentia* of Turnus is close to the *menis* (wrath) of Achilles,
and we respond to it with admiration and awe, knowing how
costly it is going to be. There are differences, though, between
Achilles and Turnus. Achilles is the hero of the *Iliad*, while
Turnus is only Aeneas's antagonist. The Achaean warrior
chooses his fate, having been offered the options of a long and
obscure life or a short but glorious one; Turnus has no such
options. Aeneas is an intruder, an interloper and a usurper,
while Turnus is the offended party—Latinus has broken what
Turnus took to be an engagement to Lavinia and given her
hand, instead, to the Trojan arriviste. When Turnus fights, we
feel that he is correct to do so, and Virgil sees to it that we are,
to a considerable degree, rooting for his hopeless cause.

Aeneas, on the other hand, is a paragon, lofty but tiresome, and what we find most exasperating about him are his
chief virtues, his dedication to his purpose and his self-con-
trol. In sharp contrast to these are Turnus's passion and spontaneity, which are appealingly human qualities, although they
are directly responsible for his defeat. At the end of book 11,
it is his impatience that causes him to abandon what might
otherwise have been a successful ambush of Aeneas and,
therefore, victory:

> In the mountain wood, meanwhile, the cruel news
> Filled Turnus' thoughts as Acca brought him word
> Of the great tumult: Volscian troops destroyed,
> Camilla fallen, foes in Mars' good graces
> Carrying all before them, riding on,
> Panic already at the city walls.
> Raging, as Jove's hard will required, Turnus
> Left the heights that he had manned and left
> The rough wood. Hardly was he out of sight
> And holding level ground, when Lord Aeneas
> Entered the pass, unguarded now, and crossed
> The ridge and issued from the woodland shade.
>
> [11.1216–27]

When, at the end of the epic, Aeneas sees that Turnus is wearing Pallas's baldric, Virgil says he "*raged* at the relic of his anguish / Worn by this man as trophy." When he kills Turnus, "his blade sinks *in fury* in Turnus' chest." He has won, has by now fulfilled his destiny, and he is no longer forced to subordinate his impulses to an epic purpose. He can afford at last to descend to the plane of ordinary human feelings and impulses and actions. He kills Turnus, but in doing so he joins—one might say that he even becomes—Turnus.

One might say that, but would it be true? Is it not putting too much weight upon *furiis* and *fervidus* to make them the fulcrum of so much of the poem's machinery? Having dreamed up an *Aeneid*, am I drawn to it, in part, no doubt, because it is my own invention? It is at least a possible alternative to the notion of the *Aeneid* as a subversively anti-Augustan document that still allows for the lack of enthusiasm one feels for Aeneas. But I am as suspicious of this reading as of the other, and I am unwilling to traduce Virgil merely for the sake of a clever critical performance. The temptation is always there to try to inscribe one's own initials this way on a piece of literary art (even to imagine posterity admiring one's discreet graffito—like Lord Byron's at Delphi). But I cannot really persuade myself that Virgil intended any such transaction between Turnus and Aeneas or such a transformation on the part of his protagonist. That he might have resolved some of the difficulties and irregularities of the poem in this way is a nice idea, but probably not Virgil's. If that had been his poem, he would almost certainly have returned our attention in those last lines from Turnus to Aeneas. But what we get is nothing like that:

He sank his blade in fury in Turnus' chest.
Then all the body slackened in death's chill,

And with a groan for that indignity
His spirit fled into the gloom below.

No sign of Aeneas anywhere! It is upon Turnus, the one we really like, the one Virgil really likes, that he keeps the tight focus.

The gestures Virgil makes elsewhere are, anyway, different, more conformable to the scale of the work and its demands for clear, broad, large strokes rather than such tiny linguistic hints and twitches as I have tried to find here. The small detail is suggestive perhaps but only interesting, in the long run, as a demonstration of my discomfort with the poem's ending. It is clear that I want in some ways to fiddle with it, to adjust it somehow, and I must assume that this dissatisfaction I feel is more or less what other attentive readers are also likely to feel.

My account of Virgil's characterization of Turnus, in particular that tessitura of his descriptive adjectives, seems persuasive enough, however. And it is true that he borrows a couple of Turnus's words and gives them to Aeneas, letting Aeneas display a little animation in his moment of triumph and in the closing lines of the epic. But the conclusion I drew from this is probably not sound. The move I fancied I saw is too modern and more likely to be my perception than Virgil's intention—which is why such an interpretation ought to be resisted—sounded perhaps (as I am doing, as I have just done) but then dismissed.

The problem then persists, though—how to deal with this recalcitrant poem in which, in the first half, Dido is more attractive than Aeneas, and in the second half, Turnus is by far the more engaging figure? The architecture of the poem is clear enough. Turnus dies by Aeneas's sword. Without pushing too hard or fetching too far, we can recall that Dido also perished on a sword, which is an unusual method of suicide for a woman. And the similarity goes beyond the two swords,

extending to the description of the release of the two spirits.
We read that Turnus's "spirit fled into the gloom below," and
are likely to recall how, in Dido's agony:

> Almighty Juno
> Filled with pity for this long ordeal
> And difficult passage, now sent Iris down
> Out of Olympus to set free
> The wrestling spirit from the body's hold.
> For since she died, not at her fated span
> Nor as she merited, but before her time
> Enflamed and driven mad, Proserpina
> Had not yet plucked from her the golden hair,
> Delivering her to Orcus of the Styx.
> So humid Iris through bright heaven flew
> On saffron-yellow wings, and in her train
> A thousand hues shimmered before the sun.
> At Dido's head she came to rest.
> "This token
> Sacred to Dis I bear away as bidden
> And free you from your body."
> Saying this,
> She cut a lock of hair. Along with it
> Her body's warmth fell into dissolution,
> And out into the winds her life withdrew.

[4.958–78]

These painstakingly executed congruencies cannot be unin-
tentional or inadvertent. They work as intricately as one of
those elaborate Swiss watches that tells not only the time but
the phases of the moon. The end of the Dido episode, moving
as it is, serves to prefigure the end of the Turnus episode and
of the entire poem. But the death of Dido is also figured in the
death of Camilla, the Volscian heroine, whose expiration in
book 11 Virgil describes: "Her spirit fled into the gloom below"—which is the line he uses again here, at the death of
Turnus. (In the Latin, there is no need for a possessive adjec-

tive, and the lines are identical: *vitaque cum gemitu fugit indig-nata sub umbras*).

One of the reasons for our sympathy for Turnus is that the fight between him and Aeneas is fixed. He knows, Turnus knows, and we do too, that Aeneas cannot lose. Virgil has done what he could to keep the poem from collapsing alto-gether by having Aeneas wounded by an arrow, but then Ve-nus miraculously intervenes, picking a stalk of dittany and invisibly descending to dip the leaves of the plant into the water with which old Iapyx, the medic, is washing the wound.

> Then, sure enough, all anguish instantly
> Left Aeneas' body, all his bleeding
> Stopped, deep in the wound. The arrowhead
> Came out, unforced and ready to his hand.
> New strength renewed his old-time fighting spirit.
>
> [12.574–577]

And in case either Aeneas or we may have missed the signif-icance of this piece of business, Iapyx prompts:

> "No mortal agency brought this about,
> No art however skilled, not my own hand
> Preserves you, but a greater power, Aeneas.
> A god is here at work. He sends you back
> To greater actions."
>
> [12.583–87]

In any western or battle movie, the convention would be for the hero to get wounded in order to show the audience his grit. He ignores the wound—it's always "just a scratch" but looks pretty bad to us, nonetheless—or he simply transcends its pain. Mezentius gives us exactly this kind of demonstration of courage and earns our respect if not our actual affection during his penultimate moments. But Aeneas's recovery, complete and instantaneous as it is, only reminds us that su-pernatural powers are at work in his behalf and that the out-come of his combat with Turnus is foreordained.

There is another kind of predestination at work in the scene, at least for those readers who have been paying attention to Virgil's deliberate echoings and transformations of Homeric tropes and turns. The last thing Turnus does is to try to pick up a large stone to heave at Aeneas, but his strength has deserted him and he can't do it. This is enough to cue a classically trained Roman reader to think of the passage in book 5 of the *Iliad* in which Diomedes is on the rampage and has all but killed Aeneas:

> But Tydeus' son in his hand caught
> up a stone, a huge thing, which no two men could carry
> such as men are now, but by himself he lightly hefted it.
> He threw, and caught Aineias in the hip, in the place
> where the hip-bone
> turns inside the thigh, the place men call the cup-socket.
> It smashed the cup-socket and broke the tendons both
> sides of it,
> and the rugged stone tore the skin backward, so that
> the fighter
> dropping to one knee stayed leaning on the ground with
> his heavy
> hand, and a covering of black night came over both eyes.
> [Lattimore, 5.302-10]

He's a dead man, for all intents and purposes, except that Aphrodite comes to the rescue, flings her arms about him, spreads a fold of her garment to shelter him against Danaan missiles, and carries him off. And enraged, Diomedes wounds Aphrodite with his spear so that she drops him and Apollo takes him up. . . .

All that comes from the reference to the stone, which is enough to summon not only the details of the encounter in the *Iliad* but to remind us that Aeneas is unlikely to be bested here. We may perhaps remember that in book 8 of the *Aeneid*, Turnus sent Venulus as his envoy to Diomedes, who is now living in Italy, to make an alliance with him, asking his aid and establishing for us one of those Virgilian pairings. When Turnus goes for the stone and finds that he can't pick it up, what we are seeing is a carefully contrived response to the famous passage in the *Iliad*. There is, then, at least a literary inevitability to the contest, and for that reason, we find it difficult to feel much suspense about the outcome or concern for Aeneas's danger. In short, it is not easy to care about the poem's hero. My impression is that Virgil had the same difficulty. But Virgil's intelligence and honesty were such that he recognized in Aeneas a dismal grandeur that is all the more depressing because he is so inexorably fated to win. We may think of Aeneas as representing the force and majesty of history, which is not so vague as it first seems. The posters of Soviet propagandists (or, indeed, the propagandists of any totalitarian regime) always featured idealized monumental heads looking boldly into the future and representing the triumph of whatever class or race or nation has come temporarily into ascendance. The family resemblance of these figures to Aeneas we must note with some discomfort. They are the stepchildren and bastards if not the legitimate heirs of Virgil's creation.

My impression is that Virgil may have understood this, that he may have even disliked Aeneas, recognizing at the same time that any expression of such dislike would have been sentimental and soft-headed. The reason for some of the contrariness of the poem may be that something in Virgil's spirit struggled against his tough-minded and clear-eyed understanding of how the world works. Realpolitik is often unpretty, as history gives us what winners it will. The only thing to do as their parades go by and as we cheer for them (it's dangerous not to) is to think of Dido and Turnus and remember what these triumphs cost.

Virgil was mindful of these costs, which is what the contrariness of the poem shows us. And if there is a meaning to the legend of Virgil's deathbed instruction that the epic be destroyed, and if that is admitted to be a part of the poem, then the text is clear, convincing, and very sad. The true meaning of the *Aeneid* does not emerge during Augustus's time, although the hints were there, but in Caligula's and Nero's—and in ours.

Virgil was not a dreamer. He was a poet of what is, reminding us of what we might rather forget—that history, or fate, or the gods do not seem to share our preferences and susceptibilities. Turnus may be a sympathetic and engaging figure, but those are trivial considerations in the real world, and epic poetry cannot afford to let itself—or us—be too much beguiled by them. Turnus is, in the end, without force or power. The nightmarish passage in which he confronts Aeneas at last makes this quite clear:

> Just as in dreams when the night-swoon of sleep
> Weighs on our eyes, it seems we try in vain
> To keep on running, try with all our might,
> But in the midst of effort faint and fail:
> Our tongue is powerless, familiar strength
> Will not hold up our body, not a sound
> Or word will come: just so with Turnus now:
> However bravely he made shift to fight
> The immortal fiend blocked and frustrated him.
> Flurrying images passed through his mind.
> He gazed at the Rutulians, and beyond them,
> Gazed at the city, hesitant, in dread.
> He trembled now before the poised spear-shaft
> And saw no way to escape; he had no force
> With which to close, or reach his foe.
>
> [12.1232–46]

Richard II is probably the most attractive, as he is surely one of the most poetic, of the characters in Shakespeare's history plays. We like him a great deal more than Henry IV, but that doesn't change how the play comes out or keep Bolingbroke from unseating Richard. The dim Boy Scout virtues Bolingbroke displays and his very lack of poetic imagination better equip him for political success than Richard's dreamy brooding. Shakespeare understood what Virgil had recognized—that because of Aeneas's narrowly focused force, his determination, and that tiresome singlemindedness, he was bound to triumph. If at the end he indulges himself for a moment and allows himself the luxury of killing the man who killed Pallas, it is because at that point it doesn't make any difference any more.

Most people encounter the *Aeneid* under some degree of compulsion somewhere along the line in school, and this circumstance has had a curiously distorting effect on the poem's career. It is at once more official and less intelligible than it might be under more normal conditions. Those students who give themselves to the poem and are willing to let it speak to them in ways that may not affect their proficiency in sight translation exercises or their performance on examinations are still at some considerable disadvantage, if only because the *Aeneid* is not a poem for young people. Their teachers may feel some affinity with it, but the youthful students are unlikely to understand Virgilian regret or to have had much occasion to experience that carefully calibrated demonstration of feeling most of us rely on to get through most of life. The series of moral burdens Aeneas has carried from the start of the poem cannot yet have weighed on their frail shoulders.

Those of us who read the poem as adults, whether going back to it out of duty or curiosity or nostalgia, or encountering it for the first time, are going to be drawn to Dido and to Turnus, as Virgil was and as he intended that we should be. But if these characters represent the limits to the cool Aeneas, he is their limit too, and the occasion for the spilling of their hotter blood. Virgil's admiration for Aeneas—and our own—may be grudging, qualified, even a little forced, but just as the reluctant Juno must give in, we too must acknowledge what the omnipotent Jove advises:

> "Come now, at last
> Have done, and heed our pleading, and give way.

> Let yourself no longer be consumed
> Without relief by all that inward burning;
> Let care and trouble not forever come to me
> From your sweet lips. The finish is at hand.
> You had the power to harry men of Troy
> By land and sea, to light the fires of war
> Beyond belief, to scar a family
> With mourning before marriage. I forbid
> Your going further."
>
> [12.1083–93]

With Juno, we must admit the world that is, whether or not it conforms to our aesthetic predilections or political preferences. Our sympathies have been—were intended to be— with Dido and Turnus, and Virgil relies on that and defies us, rubs our noses in what happens, and teaches us a lesson he understands is disagreeable.

For Jewish children who are being taught to read, teachers put a drop of honey on the page of their first book to give them a hint of the sweetness that is to come. On the first page of the *Aeneid*, there ought to be gall: "Arms and the man, I sing, who first from the shores of Troy, exiled by fate, came to Lavinia. . . ." Dido, Turnus, and all those dead bodies are, for Aeneas, so many steppingstones. He forges ahead to arrive, by the end of the poem, at an action which appears to us as very close to butchery.

If, at that point, Virgil turns his eyes and ours away from Aeneas's face, it is not simply from distaste. The gesture, I think, is also one of submission and respect.

EPILOGUE:
VIRGIL, THE MAGICIAN

THERE IS LITERARY WORTH, WHICH IS ONE THING. THERE IS ALSO
the independent working of the wheel of Fortuna, which is
quite another. The reputation of a poet prospers or languishes
in ways that are quite mysterious. The prosperity of Virgil has
been prodigious, even if we make allowance for the preemi-
nence of his accomplishment. He was always fortunate, which
is no bad thing. When someone remarked disparagingly of
one of Napoleon's successful generals that he had been less
smart than lucky, Napoleon is supposed to have answered
that he was happy to settle for that.

Virgil's achievement was very great, but that doesn't entirely explain the legends that grew up in the Middle Ages
about his magical powers and that brought him into the Renaissance as rather a spooky figure—to whom it was only reasonable for Dante to look when he needed a guide to the
mysteries of Hell. One can look at *Eclogues* 4 and 8 and see in
the one a prediction of the coming of Christ and in the other
a mini-treatise on magic. One can also adduce the visit to the
underworld in book 6 of the *Aeneid* and take that as a kind of
qualifying credential for Virgil's supernatural powers, even
though it was Anchises who was predicting the future rather
than Virgil himself. These mysterious powers don't match the
texts exactly, or even have much to do with them at all. But
they were enough to allow for superstitious reverence. Virgil's
accomplishments as a poet and his reputation as a wise man
may have been the prerequisite for the odd flight of his reputation, but they are not enough to explain how that reputa-

tion took off and developed according to its own peculiar logic.

John Webster Spargo offered a compendium of these legends and tall tales in *Virgil the Necromancer*, and it is worth setting down a few of the more picturesque of these stories to suggest something of the irrationality of fame and its devices. That Virgil was a very great poet did not necessarily imply any magic powers, but among the marvels and wonders that were attributed to him in a widespread series of texts are:

- The ability to rid a region of pests. Virgil is said to have ended a visitation of bloodsucking leeches by throwing a golden leech into a well. He is also said to have helped the butchers, whose meat was spoiling, by enclosing the meat market with a wall of air, which he accomplished by using the power of some herb. The effect was to keep meat perfectly preserved for as long as five hundred years.
- The Virgilian garden. This was protected by "immobile air." In the garden were wooden statues, each of which held a bell in its hand and represented one of the Empire's provinces. In the event of trouble in any of these provinces, the representative statue would ring its bell, and a bronze horseman on top of his palace would point his spear in the direction of the trouble.
- Virgil's bones. These were said to have been kept in a castle that overlooked the Bay of Naples and was surrounded by the sea. When the bones were exposed to the air, there would be terrible storms that would subside when the bones were covered again.
- Healing waters. There were fountains Virgil turned into medicinal baths at Pozzuoli with the power to cure a variety of illnesses. After Virgil's death, the labels of these medicinal springs were destroyed by the local physicians, who objected that they were interfering with their business. People could no longer be certain which waters cured what illnesses and had then to proceed by trial and error.

These entertaining stories, appealing as they are in their fairy-tale simplicity, seem to have rather little to do with the sophisticated literary productions we have been considering. There can be no doubt, however, that they contributed to the prosperity of Virgil's reputation during the medieval period. And their aura of the fabulous, that peculiar dazzle and shimmer, is not just a distraction but can be helpful to us. Keeping in mind how these stories seem to cross the borders of religious and literary domains, we may try to read the poems not simply as modern "texts" but as readers have done in cultural and historical situations quite different from our own. The poems have their own histories and careers, odd encrustations we ought not ignore.

Just for comparison, we might think of modern physicists. There can be no question about the achievements and contributions of Einstein, but were they, after all, of a whole different order from those of Nils Bohr, Enrico Fermi, Robert Millikan, or Werner Heisenberg, none of whom has managed to make the peculiar transition from a mere eminence in physics to membership in the pantheon of popular figures who regularly appear on T-shirts, coffee mugs, greeting cards, and the paraphernalia of kitsch?

Professor Spargo is more concerned with providing a complete and even encyclopedic enumeration of the bizarre stories about Virgil than with offering explanations about how these stories came into being, but he does make some suggestive observations here and there. One of these—which seems to me quite plausible—is that, in 972, an Arabic chronicler writes of the Sicilians that there was a mosque in Palermo, formerly a church, in which the bones of Aristotle were said to lie in a wooden box hanging in the sanctuary:

> The Christians greatly honored the tomb of this philosopher, and used to invoke rain from him, believing the tradition left by the ancient Greeks about his great excellence in intellectual matters. The logician said that the box

was always suspended there in mid-air, because the people would run to pray for rain, or for the public safety, and for deliverance from all of the calamities which induce man to turn to God and propitiate Him; such things happen in times of famine, pestilence, or civil war. In truth I saw up there a great box of wood and perhaps it contained the tomb.

It is Spargo's observation—which he bases in part on F. W. Hasluck's *Letters on Religion and Folklore* (Luzac, 1926)—that if Aristotle's bones were protecting Palermo, then Naples, which was Palermo's enemy, also probably needed a similar set of protective bones. Among the Neapolitans Virgil would have been as likely a candidate as anyone. Roger II, the Norman king of Palermo, is said to have sent an Englishman as his agent to try to steal Virgil's bones. (Or this may simply be a story fabricated in Naples for home consumption in order to reassure the Neapolitans that the power of their tutelary genius was acknowledged by the enemy, and that therefore they could believe in it themselves.)

Cultural emblems of this kind have to begin somewhere, and the mechanics of these beginnings, random and happenstance as they are, may be forgotten even by the people for whom the emblems are alive. The "bullpen" in which relief pitchers warm up in baseball parks takes its name from the sign for Bull Durham tobacco that used to hang in Yankee Stadium out there where the pitchers loosened up (and the bull on the sign came from the Coleman's mustard label that the owner of the Bull Durham company had always admired and had adopted for his own logo). The term caught on and spread to other parks and fields and stadiums—where nobody even thinks to question it.

The power of Virgil's bones to stir up or to calm the seas seems quaint to us because the utility of saints' relics is no longer a part of the official culture and has been relegated to the private sector of superstition and folk belief. We go, nevertheless, to inspect the writing table of Longfellow or admire Dickens's inkwell still showing that odd shade of bright blue from the ink he liked, and we try to extrude somehow whatever it is that inheres in the gloves Napoleon is supposed to have worn at Waterloo that are now on display in a museum case in Milan. . . . But we don't quite admit to ourselves (let alone anyone else) that these mere objects have power.

The notion that the remains of Aristotle were suspended in a box in that sanctuary is a curious one, which suggests a whole range of stories Spargo adduces about Virgil hanging in a basket. Lots of people are suspended in baskets as a public humiliation that is either itself a punishment or may be associated with some other, more severe punishment. And the punished person may or may not exact a revenge. The earliest appearance of Virgil in one of these stories is in a thirteenth-century Latin manuscript in the Bibliothèque Nationale in Paris, of which an extract was printed by Edelstand Duméril in *Mélanges archéologiques et littéraires* (1850):

> Virgil is enamoured of Nero's beautiful daughter and begs for her love. She invites him to appear at night at the foot of her tower, where, divested of his clothing, he enters a basket which she has lowered, is pulled up halfway and left suspended until the next day. The news gets about even to the emperor, who is greatly enraged and, following the custom of the times, passes sentence of death upon Virgil. The magician makes his escape to Naples by muttering an incantation over a basin of water, and then exacts his revenge.

That Virgil was never in love with Nero's daughter and didn't live to see Nero assume the purple is irrelevant. The important point is that, as Spargo correctly suggests, "the basket story was floating about and was likely to be attached to almost any name that happened to come into the relater's mind." He cites a fourteenth-century diatribe against women in which the basket adventure is related as having befallen, in one way or another, Adam, Solomon, Helen, Charlemagne, Samson, Pasiphaë, and Dido, among others. There are versions in *A Thousand and One Nights*, but without the revenge element. The attribution to Virgil, however adventitious it may first have been, did stick somehow and persisted for some centuries through to modern times. Anatole France referred to it in *L'Ile des pingouins*, in which Frère Marbode is warned by a fellow monk against the dangers of reading Virgil because he was a magician and, in spite of his power, was deceived by a courtesan of Naples who pulled him up and left him suspended in a basket used to pull up provisions.

What has any of this to do with Virgil? Strictly speaking, nothing whatever. But we never speak as strictly as we might like and, as Freud demonstrated for us, it is often in our lapses and our jokes that we give and receive hints about urgent and very serious matters. It seems to me that the revenge motif in these stories fits in with the notions about Virgil's ability to perform various kinds of magic. The darker aspects of magic are those we fear, those that may be used against us. We admire the supernatural that is beneficent and protective, but there is a recognition in these stories of the double edge of that sword. Virgil is elevated but he is naked, a figure for ridicule and derision, and it is for this insult that he can turn nasty, exacting punishment from those who have discommoded him. With his occult powers, he extinguishes all the fires in Rome (the idea of fire was perhaps sufficient to have suggested Nero to one of these early fabulists) and the people are famished because they can't cook. The emperor begs Virgil for relief and the reply is that the fires can be restored only if the emperor's daughter, who has humiliated Virgil, will expose herself naked in the marketplace and let the people light their torches and candles by touching them to her body. The enchantment will continue, Virgil warns, until every person in Rome has visited her, because one torch will not be able to light another.

We respond to this as we do to any satisfying children's story, lowering our guard a little and allowing the masked but still discernible emotions to play themselves out. We recognize certain fundamental truths, I think, in the dramatic reversal of the story. It is not necessary to be a great poet to have experienced the combination of admiration and envy a bright child is likely to encounter among his peers and classmates in school. Virgil, the sage and mage, becomes a vessel for that kind of ambivalent feeling, and his suspension in midair is a metaphoric statement of his superiority. The populace looks up to him, but the quality of their regard is not altogether friendly.

The medieval readership for a body of sophisticated works in Latin was minuscule compared to the audience for these stories, exempla, and fabliaux. What had begun as a perfectly reasonable reputation for excellence and intelligence took off, developed its own momentum, and began to have a career of its own, with only the most indirect reference to its literary and historical source.

When Dante came to write *The Divine Comedy*, then, and wanted a guide to the mysteries of the afterlife, Virgil was standing there, not merely available but obviously qualified by his talents as a magician, with on the one hand his spooky reputation as a kind of pre-Christian prophet and, on the other, his slightly eerie aura as a worker of wonders, fortune-teller, necromancer, mystagogue, and general dabbler in occult arts. Dante could not have spent much time trying to find among the classical poets any likelier guide for his venture. Virgil, the paradigmatic poet-magus, was the one obvious choice for such a role. Dante makes no reference to that aspect of Virgil's reputation, does not describe him as a magician or as a pagan John the Baptist, but only as a *poet*, and the effect, I think, is quite simply and effortlessly to imply that all poets are, by the very nature of what they do, seers.

During the course of their first encounter, Dante expresses doubts about his worthiness and his strength to visit

these forbidden precincts, "Io non Enëa, io non Paolo sono: /
me degno a ciò nè io nè altri crede" (I am not Aeneas, I am
not Paul: / neither I nor any man thinks me fit for this.) Virgil
reassures him, saying

> Da questa tema acciò che tu ti solve,
>   dirotti perch' io venni e quel ch' io 'ntesi
>   nel primo punto che di te mi dolve.
> Io era tra color che son sospesi,
>   e donna mi chiamò beata e bella,
>   tal che di comandare io la richiesi.
>   [*Inferno* 2.49–54]

[That I may deliver you from this fear, I shall tell you
why I came and what I heard at the time when I first took
pity on you. I was among those who are in suspense,
and a lady called me, so blessed and so fair that I begged
her to command me.]

The usual and correct interpretation of *sospesi*, or "suspended,"
is that Virgil was among those who were hanging in Limbo.
But the Virgil-in-the-basket is also "suspended," dangling
awkwardly between earth and heaven, and this iconographic
representation was sufficiently widespread as to be his device.
As St. Jerome is always shown with a lion, or St. Honoré with
a baker's peel, Virgil has his basket; representations of some
figure hanging from a tower in a basket adorn many of the
title pages of the early printings of his poetry. It is more than
likely that Dante had taken this image and transformed it into
an emblem of Virgil's theological and eschatological predicament.

To have been adopted by the supreme poet of the Italian
Renaissance as the sage and guide for his Easter weekend pil-
grimage and exploration of the ultimate mysteries was surely
a good thing for the prosperity of Virgil's reputation and that
of his writings. Similarly, any sane or sensible person in Virgil's time, in the Rome of Augustus Caesar, could hardly have

expected that those barbaric tribes of the north in Germany and Britain would develop an educational and class system eighteen hundred years later that would require the study of Latin and use it as a means of gatekeeping for entrance to pre- ferred jobs in the professions and the civil service. But this is the kind of luck Virgil has always had—and to have been this lucky for this long is a kind of magic to which we must give not only our assent but our amazed admiration.

There are too many poets. Or, more accurately, society has grown too large, too complicated. Back in some earlier and simpler time, one can imagine small groups of nomadic tribes- men or settled villagers, and in each group there would be a poet, a story-teller or bard whose job it would be to remember and retell the great events. Along with the shaman and the medicine man, the poet had his function, and there were ritual occasions when people would gather around the fire to hear him chant or intone in whatever style he had inherited the story of the raid on the next village, or the killing of the moose, or the life and death of the old king.

We gather now around a television screen and hear Dan Rather and Tom Brokaw and Peter Jennings tell us in their more or less crisp way, with appropriate illustrative photo- graphs, what the executives have decided is the significant news of the day. Poets have been driven ever more inward, to explore the terrain of their secret souls, even as their au- diences have been agglomerated into larger and larger units. There is no tribe or family or village to speak to any more, but each poet must address his whole civilization, must try to make his or her voice heard above the deafening babble. For any poet to be able to do that requires a lot of luck, and per- haps more luck than talent.

In *The Alexandria Quartet*, Lawrence Durrell refers to Ca- vafy as "the old poet of the city." That is no mean thing, to speak for a city, for a time and place. But I am afraid we now ask even more than that of our poets. We demand of them that they speak to all men and women, of all times and places. And while that expectation is nearly impossible, there are some voices so loud, so fortunately timbred and pitched, that they seem to be able to do that.

"The poet?"

A few names come to mind. Homer, of course. And then? Virgil, Dante, and Shakespeare.

Virgil is the only one on the list who appears as a character in the work of one of the others.

He was Dante's guide to the underworld, and Sigmund Freud's as well, for on the title page of the first edition of *Die Traumdeutung* (The interpretation of dreams), just below the abbreviated name of the author ("Dr. Sigm. Freud"), there is a line of Latin—"Flectere se nequeo superos, Acheronta movebo"—without attribution. (But, as Freud pointed out, omissions and silences are often louder than declarations.)

The line is Virgil's, from the *Aeneid* (7.312), and it is Juno who is speaking, saying, "If I cannot bend the gods, I will stir up Acheron [the underworld]."

SELECTED BIBLIOGRAPHY

The best way to read Virgil obviously is in the original Latin, but the teaching of Latin seems to be designed to discourage more than to attract students. Latin and Greek are actually easier to learn than the living languages because they do not require so keenly developed a sense of nuance, do not depend on *Sprachgefühl,* and demand only that—in the words of a teacher of mine long ago—one be "not immune to the pleasures of memorization." This would get a small laugh, but he would go on to explain that memorization did indeed have its pleasures and that it was the only form of intellectual challenge that yielded reliably to effort.

Still, young men and women were made to wade through a year of grammar, another year of Caesar's forced marches of many thousands of paces (crossing those bridges-resting-on-piles, and then, once again, pitching camp), and then a year of Cicero's speeches ("How long, O Cicero, are we to endure your maunderings here in the Senate?"). That curriculum has been modified in recent years, although not necessarily improved—Caesar fell from favor during the Vietnam era, and there is some Livy or Petronius or Apuleius that gets thrown in to leaven the Cicero now, but the poetry is still kept as a reward for long service, the idea being that the good students will be those who survive the earlier hurdles. Actually, many of the best students have been driven away—as I was. A few of us return later, though, to snatch the forbidden goodies that have been withheld, feeling that we are trespassing, that we have skipped to the dessert (the poetry) without having eaten all of our Brussels sprouts (the prose). We have the delicious sense that we are naughty children.

For such students, the reading of Virgil in Latin needs some help. The Loeb Classical Library Virgil—with H. R. Fairclough's rendering—is adequate, and the colorlessness of the translation has at

least the virtue of not distracting from what is going on *en face* in the
Latin verses. If one is able to obtain one of the really wicked and
forbidden books, though, one can use a real Virgil—the Macmillan/
St Martin's *Aeneid* in two volumes, edited and with notes by R. D.
Williams (1972 and 1973) is admirable and widely available—and a
student's interlinear trot. I have a 1966 David McKay reprint of an
1882 interlinear translation by Levi Hart and V. R. Osborn of the
Aeneid, and of the *Eclogues* and the *Georgics* by Hart alone, in a compact and convenient volume. It isn't elegant or pretentious, but it
does what one wants it to do. With this and the Williams, almost
anyone can read Virgil more or less in the original. The only other
book one might need would be something like Roger Hornsby's *Reading Latin Poetry* (University of Oklahoma Press, 1967) for a discussion
of how the metrics work—although any Latin grammar will have a
short section on metrics which, after some practice, will yield itself.
      My interlinear begins:

> **Cano arma que virum qui profugus fato, primus venit**
> I sing, arms and the hero who driven by fate first has come
> **ab oris Trojae Italiam que Lavinia littora**
> from the coasts of Troy to Italy and the Lavinian shores:
> **multum ille jactatus et terris et alto vi superum**
> much he *has been* tossed both on land and on the sea by the
>   power of the gods above,
> **ob memorem iram saevae Junonis. . . .**
> on account of the lasting wrath of cruel Juno

With that kind of thing in one hand, it is not difficult to read the Latin
verses:

> Arma virumque cano, Troiae qui primus ab oris
> Italiam fato profugus, Laviniaque venit
> litora, multum ille et terris iactatus et alto
> vi superum saevae memorem Iunonis ob iram. . . .

You do that long enough, and you find yourself learning Latin—
which is one of the desirable outcomes of translation. Nabokov's rendering of *Eugene Onegin* is, in fact, a course in Russian in a not altogether persuasive disguise.
      There will be those for whom the Latin is either too troublesome
or for whom it will be an actual occasion for allergic attack, hives,
and an uncertain feeling in the stomach and diaphragm. And for

them, there are a number of translations into English. As with everything else, Virgil has been fortunate in his translators. The invention
of English blank verse comes from the work of Henry Howard, earl
of Surrey, in around 1540, who did books 2 and 4 of the *Aeneid*.
O. B. Hardison's truly magisterial *Prosody and Purpose in the English
Renaissance* (Johns Hopkins University Press, 1989) has a chapter devoted to Surrey's work, its relation to Gavin Douglas's earlier version, as well as to Thomas Caxton's prose *Eneydos* of 1490, and the
ways in which Surrey's metrical practice was later misunderstood.

At the other end of the long line of renditions of Virgil's work
into English stands the Robert Fitzgerald *Aeneid* (Random House,
1983; Vintage Books paperback edition, 1984), which I like and have
cited in my discussions in this volume. What I admire most about
this translation is that it is faithful to Virgil's tone—about which I
have my reservations. Rolfe Humphries's version (Scribners, 1951),
C. Day Lewis's (Oxford University Press, 1952), and Patrick Dick-
inson's (New American Library, 1961) all seem too chatty, colloquial,
or conversational, as if they were trying to tame Virgil, scale him
down, and bring him back from his off-putting excesses. Allan Mandelbaum's version (University of California Press, 1981) would probably
be my second choice. Fitzgerald and, to a lesser extent, Mandelbaum
manage to suggest the resonance of Virgil, offering a kind of grandiloquence that never sounds totally ridiculous, and this is no mean
feat. The good parts they get right, too, but the way to judge translators and translations is sometimes to look at their improvisations
at those places that are less than wonderful. Those other translations
tend to be cozier and more *convenable*, and that is, for some readers,
a significant advantage. They are all reliable and one should look for
what one finds comfortable, for it is better to have read a tamed and
slightly distorted *Aeneid* than none at all. For those who are allergic
to poetry in all forms and want an accurate, inoffensive prose version, I suppose W. F. Jackson Knight's Penguin edition (revised,
1958) will serve as well as any.

The *Eclogues* and the *Georgics* present another kind of challenge.
They don't depend so much on narrative and drama and are, therefore, more languagy works and consequently harder to do into English. Smith Palmer Bovie's *Georgics* (University of Chicago Press,
1956; Phoenix paperback edition, 1966) is very close to the Latin and
quite readable, as is that of Robert Wells (Carcanet, 1982). L. P. Wilkinson has a curious version out in Penguin (1982) in which *Georgic*

2 begins: "Thus far my song has been of tilth below / And stars above. . . ." One must at least admire his nerve.

The old E. V. Rieu Penguin Classics version of the *Eclogues* (1949) is in prose and offers useful essays on each of the poems. The newer Penguin, Guy Lee's version (1984), is in verse with the Latin on facing pages (as Rieu's was not) and seems attractive, although I slightly prefer, or at least am habituated to, the Day Lewis *Eclogues and Georgics of Virgil* (Anchor Books, 1964), which had both works with the Latin opposite. To defy consistency, I must admit that my favorite version of the *Georgics* is John Dryden's, which is in couplets and therefore takes some liberties with Virgil, but is surprisingly close to the meaning of the Latin and is, mainly, successful *as a poem*—which is, after all, the first and most important objective. Here is how Dryden begins:

What makes a plenteous harvest, when to turn
The fruitful soil, and when to sow the corn;
The care of sheep, of oxen, and of kine;
And how to raise on elms the teeming vine;
The birth and genius of the frugal bee,
I sing, Maecenas, and I sing to thee.
Ye dieties! who fields and plains protect,
Who rule the seasons, and the year direct,
Bacchus and fostering Ceres, powers divine,
Who gave us corn for mast, for water, wine:
Ye Fauns, propitious to the rural swains,
Ye Nymphs that haunt the mountains and the plains,
Join in my work, and to my numbers bring
Your needful succor; for your gifts I sing.

In his remarks about the difficulties of translating Racine, Richard Wilbur has suggested that it is difficult to write seriously in couplets. The form tends to provoke an uneasy laughter—which can be useful if you're doing Molière but is something to be overcome in unfunny, not to mention tragic, passages. Dryden's suave assurance in couplets not only succeeds in this difficult transcendence but actually helps the Virgil I have in mind, for the art and the labor of the undertaking are always evident, and the muscularity of the struggle is clear with each graceful rhyme which he wrests from a rhyme-poor language. Dryden's *Aeneid* seems to me perhaps too suave and too engaging. The scale is changed with the pinging of those clockwork rhymes. This is agreeable, and surely worth reading for itself, but not what I think of as Virgil's *Aeneid*. One ought at least to take a look. It starts out:

> Arms and the Man I sing, who, forced by Fate,
> And haughty Juno's unrelenting hate,
> Expelled and exiled, left the Trojan shore.
> Long labors both by land and sea he bore,
> And in the doubtful war, before he won
> The Latian realm, and built the destined town. . . .

It is astonishingly accomplished, although it does curious things to the epic. In the *Georgics* it works extraordinarily well and is, for my money, unbeatable.

I suppose I ought to mention my own versions of the *Eclogues* and *Georgics* that Doubleday published almost twenty years ago and that have been reissued in paperback by Johns Hopkins University Press (1990). These are even more free (some would say reckless) than Dryden's renditions, but the intention is not dissimilar. I too was trying for readable poems, part translations and part meditations on the original works. Judgments about the degree of success of this enterprise and whether it was worth the costs (in terms of fidelity) are best left to others, but I may say on behalf of my old work that the original poems were and still are available, and that if I was traducing them more than translating them, I was at least calling attention to them with what I hope comes across as lively enthusiasm. I cite a typically outrageous passage, the beginning of *Georgic* 4:

> To bee or not to . . .
> > > > > > Never mind. Forget it!
> It isn't the time yet for fooling around.
> Still, to have got this far . . .
> > > > > > > > And five hundred lines
> on bees? It shouldn't be hard.
>
>
> > > > > I will do it, sir.
> Not for the money, which I acknowledge with thanks,
> nor even the fame which I shouldn't at all mind,
> but because I can, because I can see it now,
> all of it, all the way, and am amazed,
> myself, at what I have done, am doing, will do . . .
> The greatest of labor's rewards may be such moments,
> not at the very end, but nearing, nearing,

when you look back and ahead, and you feel able.
Sweeter than honey, Maecenas.

Even the drones
(like you and me) must quiver to that buzz,
the feel of the prospering hive, the work, the wonder
of flourishing, of community, of order.

Those who wish to read further and at least sample some of the voluminous body of criticism and scholarship that Virgil's work has occasioned might wish to begin with the useful collections of essays that have been assembled by Harold Bloom (Chelsea House, Modern Critical Views Series, 1986) or Steele Commager (*Virgil: A Collection of Critical Essays* [Prentice-Hall, 1966]). Bloom also has a volume of essays devoted entirely to the *Aeneid* (Chelsea House, 1987).

Among the essays I have found to be useful, either informative or at least provocative, there are, first of all, the views of two modern poets:

Robert Graves's assertively wrong-headed Oxford lecture on Virgil as "the anti-poet," in *Robert Graves on Poetry: Collected Talks and Essays* (Doubleday, 1969). This cranky and intemperate piece was what led me to begin translating Virgil in the first place.

And T. S. Eliot's peculiar consideration of Virgil in *On Poets and Poetry* (Farrar Straus, 1957).

Other, more scholarly, and sometimes more reliable views are to be found in:

G. E. Duckworth's *Structural Patterns and Proportions in Vergil's "Aeneid"* (University of Michigan Press, 1962).

Philip Hardie's *Virgil's* Aeneid: *Cosmos and Imperium* (Oxford University Press, 1986; Clarendon Press paperback edition, 1989).

W. F. Jackson Knight's *Roman Vergil* (Barnes and Noble, 1971).

W. R. Johnson's *Darkness Visible: A Study of Vergil's "Aeneid"* (University of California Press, 1976).

Eleanor Winsor Leach's *Virgil's* Eclogues (Cornell University Press, 1974).

Sara Mack's *Patterns of Time in Vergil* (Archon Books, 1978).

Gregory Nagy's *The Best of the Achaeans* (Johns Hopkins University Press, 1979).

Brooks Otis's *Virgil: A Study in Civilized Poetry* (Oxford University Press, 1963).

Michael C. J. Putnam's *The Poetry of the Aeneid* (Harvard University Press, 1965;, Cornell University Press paperback edition, 1988).

John Webster Spargo's *Virgil the Necromancer: Studies in Virgilian Legends* (Harvard University Press, 1934).

L. P. Wilkinson's *The Georgics of Virgil: A Critical Survey* (Cambridge University Press, 1969)

Gordon Williams's *Tradition and Originality in Roman Poetry* (Oxford University Press, 1968); *Figures of Thought in Roman Poetry* (Yale University Press, 1980); and *Technique and Ideas in the "Aeneid"* (Yale University Press, 1983).

R. D. Williams's *The Aeneid* (Allen & Unwin, 1987).

Raymond Williams's *The Country and the City* (Oxford University Press, 1973).

INDEX

DATE DUE

JAN 2 5 1995			
MAR 3 0 1996			

Demco, Inc. 38-293